Stewardship of our God-endowed feelings affects every part of our lives. In *Your Spiritual and Emotional Power,* Dr. Richard D. Dobbins addresses an important responsibility — and potential benefit — of this stewardship: *mental health.* Drawing from his twenty-six years as a pastor and nearly twenty years as a clinical psychologist, Dr. Dobbins describes how the behavioral sciences can help you apply God's wisdom to your life situations in ways that are consistent with Scripture. He examines specific emotional concerns and shows you how to recognize them, understand them, accept them, control them, and use them constructively. This guide to developing healthy faith and feelings will enrich your personal life and improve your interpersonal relationships.

YOUR SPIRITUAL and EMOTIONAL POWER

Richard D. Dobbins

Power Books

Fleming H. Revell Company
Old Tappan, New Jersey

Scripture quotations in this volume are from the King James Version.

Permission to quote in this volume from previously published material is gratefully acknowledged:

Chapter 1 is a revised version of *The Believer and His Mental Health,* © 1982 by Dr. Richard D. Dobbins. Chapters 2–6 have been adapted from material in the film series, "The Believer and His Mental Health," © 1982 by Dr. Richard D. Dobbins/Totally Alive Publications. Chapter 7 was originally published under the title, *How an Ordinary Person Can Enjoy an Extraordinary Life,* © 1982 by Dr. Richard D. Dobbins.

Library of Congress Cataloging in Publication Data

Dobbins, Richard D.
    Your spiritual and emotional power.

    "Power book."
    1. Christian life—1960–   . 2. Emotions—Religious aspects—Christianity. I. Title.
BV4501.2D593   1984   248.4   83-26969
ISBN 0-8007-5136-1 (pbk.)

ACKNOWLEDGMENTS

I would like to express appreciation to my wife and family for their patience in tolerating my preoccupation with the task of preparing this manuscript. A special thanks should also go to Mrs. Carol Adams for her editorial assistance. I would also like to thank Mr. Fritz Ridenour for his creative suggestions.

In any venture of this nature, one is indebted to so many that he is reluctant to mention any for fear of implying that the efforts of those not mentioned are unappreciated. I hope those thoughtful enough to read this expression are kind enough to avoid such a conclusion.

CONTENTS

FOREWORD

Our feelings about ourselves, our families, and life in general were formed long before we developed any conscious God-awareness. The spiritual experience each has grows out of his earlier realities and is affected by them.

Therefore, the emotional and spiritual dimensions of our lives are closely related. Each impacts upon the other and interacts with it in affecting other dimensions of our global reality. This book is written to help us understand the nature of that interaction more clearly.

Mental illness and emotional disturbance may distort one's view of God, self, and others. On the other hand, a healthy spiritual experience can be an effective therapeutic resource for the mentally ill and emotionally disturbed in their efforts to regain their mental health.

When our spiritual experience and religious beliefs are consistent with healthy views of God, self, and others, they help minimize our emotional pain and maximize our pleasures in life. The author hopes this book will assist the reader in reaching this goal.

The illustrations used throughout the book are descriptive of people with whom I have counseled. Names, circumstances, and other identifying data have been altered to conceal identities.

PREFACE

This book addresses one of the most important responsibilities and potential benefits of our Christian stewardship: our mental health.

The quality of our lives as Christians affects the credibility of our testimony. A vibrant, healthy faith in Christ should be expressed in a celebration of life that is obvious to the people with whom we live and work. "The kingdom of God is not meat and drink; but righteousness, and peace, and joy in the Holy Ghost" (Romans 14:17). Professing this kingdom without enjoying it is the pathetic plight of many who have not yet discovered the vital link between spiritual experience and mental health.

The Bible says we are made in the image of God. Those same Scriptures reveal God to be One who feels as well as thinks. Being made in His image, then, means that we are *feeling* persons as well as *thinking* persons. In fact, you and I experience life through our feelings and our thoughts. However, we have been taught to pay much more attention to our thoughts than to our feelings. We have few opportunities to learn how to live with our feelings. This is in contrast to the fact that we spend much of our early years in schools primarily devoted to teaching us how to think.

More and more, pastors and church leaders are seeing the tremendous need for us to have a clearer understanding of our feelings and to develop biblical ways of expressing them. As a result, the church is slowly awakening to its role in providing us opportunities to learn about our feelings and how to live with them.

The stewardship of our feelings affects every relationship. This is true whether we are male or female, young or old, mar-

11

ried or single. Learning the origins of our feelings, becoming aware of them, and developing biblical ways of managing them cannot help but enrich our personal lives and benefit our interpersonal relationships.

This book introduces you to a relationship between faith and mental health. First, we'll look at some ways a healthy faith in God will enable you to develop and maintain healthy ways of dealing with life in general. Then, over the next five chapters, we will deal with specific problem areas that I have seen trouble God's people again and again in the more than thirty years I have spent counseling Christians. These are emotional concerns that give all of us problems from time to time: our self-concept, fear, anger, guilt, and depression. Of these five, a poor self-concept is perhaps the most common. Often this particular problem area results from improperly presented and/or poorly understood religious training during childhood. We address this issue in Chapter 2.

Then we approach the subject of fear, which also has its roots in early childhood. Fear and anxiety are the first emotions we experience as infants.

Anger, our next topic, is particularly difficult for many Christians to accept because they believe that any expression of anger is a contradiction of their faith. Nevertheless, we frequently see people from a broad segment of the church whose problems include angry abuse of their mate or their children. However, anger doesn't have to present the believer with such an overwhelming challenge. It can be a positive, healthy force in his or her life. But it has to be properly managed. And I'll make some suggestions about how this can be done.

Conscience and guilt make society possible. However, guilt can be healthy or unhealthy. There are some distinct differences between these two kinds of guilt. In Chapter 5 we'll look at both kinds and talk about how to identify and resolve each one.

In Chapter 6 we will explore ways believers can manage their bouts with depression. This is the most common of all emotional problems and afflicts an estimated fifty million Americans annually. Many of them are believers. Although the stress of modern living certainly has contributed to the present epidemic proportions of depression, it is not new or unique to our generation. Depression has been with us since Bible times.

I have seen many Christian men and women for counseling who were so depressed that they had tried to take their own life in response to a tragic situation. Others are troubled by chronic depression that has its roots in less clearly recognizable things. Still others suffer from depression that is biochemical in nature. But faith in God, coupled with the best information available from the behavioral sciences, can help the believer deal more constructively with these troublesome times.

The final chapter, "You Can Live in a New Dimension," explains a marvelous process by which we can bring our confusion and hurts to God in prayer for the guidance and healing we need. Some of the most remarkable emotional healings I have ever witnessed—or experienced—have come through times of private, personal prayer.

The behavioral sciences serve to help the believer discover practical ways for applying God's wisdom to life situations—ways that are consistent with His Word. In the final analysis, wisdom—wherever it is found—is of God. All truth is God's truth. We have His Word on that. "For the Lord giveth wisdom: out of his mouth cometh knowledge and understanding" (Proverbs 2:6).

It is my hope that this book will help you to discover healthier ways of living with your feelings through a practical application of a healthy faith in God.

Richard D. Dobbins, Ph.D.

YOUR
SPIRITUAL
and
EMOTIONAL
POWER

1

How Healthy Is Your Faith?

In its 1978 report, the President's Commission on Mental Health warned that if present trends continue, one in seven people now living in the United States will require treatment for some kind of emotional disturbance during his or her lifetime.

Why has our national environment become so threatening to our mental health? Let's look at some of the factors. Advances in science, technology, and industry have brought modern man such rapid means of transportation and communication that he may be exposed to as many life experiences in a year as previous generations knew in a lifetime. We stagger under the impact of stimulation overload.

For example, many of us travel twenty miles to work each day. After a round trip of forty miles and working eight hours, we may go out with family or friends in the evening. But back in 1900, just traveling forty miles would have consumed the entire day.

Before we had radio and television, news of events at a distance took weeks to reach us. And even then, our grasp of their reality was limited to the vivid imagery of a reporter's printed account of what happened. Today, all of the bad news of our world is delivered to our homes each morning and evening in sound and living color.

The speed of life, the rapid rate of change, the almost endless variety of options from which we may choose a life-style, the anonymous quality of our rootless society where half of the population moves every five years—these are some of the factors which combine to plague us with moral confusion and conflict. In the midst of this, we attempt to give our lives meaning and direction.

We live in a sick society

Is it any wonder that a veritable flood of emotional disturbance is sweeping across America? Each year well over fifty million people suffer from mild to moderate depression. Another two million are deeply depressed; twenty million are neurotic; ten million have serious alcohol problems; ten million have been arrested for crimes; six million children and youth are emotionally disturbed; one million students withdraw from school because of emotional problems; one million are actively schizophrenic; two hundred thousand attempt suicide; two hundred thousand cases of child abuse occur. Suicide is now the second highest cause of death among our teenagers.

In their frantic efforts to cope with this unparalleled stress, increasing numbers of Americans are turning to some form of substance abuse. I am not exaggerating when I say that every day, tons of tranquilizers, antidepressants, antipsychotic agents, and sleeping pills are being consumed by troubled people in our society.

It should be understood that psychotropic (mood-altering) drugs, properly administered and supervised by physicians, do play a legitimate role as temporary supports for people under stress. However, many people are seeking a permanent solution to their emotional problems in medication and other abused substances.

Believers are not immune to the emotional risks of our society. In fact, in the New Testament, Paul warns readers about the dangers of the crumbling social and emotional climate of the last days. He writes, in 2 Timothy 3:1–4,

> *This know also, that in the last days perilous times shall come. For men shall be lovers of their own selves, covet-*

18

*ous, boasters, proud, blasphemers, disobedient to parents,
unthankful, unholy, without natural affection, truce-
breakers, false accusers, incontinent, fierce, despisers of
those that are good, traitors, heady, highminded, lovers
of pleasure more than lovers of God.*

In the past, ministers and psychologists tended to view their
respective fields as being like oil and water. Religion and psychology, according to many of them, just didn't mix. Some still feel
that way.

Today, however, there is evidence that an increasing number
of reputable people from both camps are looking at their old
viewpoint with a careful eye. They are beginning to see the benefit of helping the minister better understand the emotional
issues involved in a person's religious experience, and of helping
the psychologist better understand the spiritual issues involved in
a person's emotional life.

Because they affect us eternally, the issues of our faith are
much more important to us than the psychological issues of life.
Nevertheless, we need all the help both fields can provide in our
effort to stay mentally healthy in our sick society.

Your faith and emotions intertwine

When I began my Christian life as a teenager, mental health
was certainly not one of my major concerns. As far as I knew, I
had grown up in a normal family. Both of my parents had been
active in church all of my life.

At that time, I simply didn't understand how good Christian
people could have emotional problems. The prevailing belief was
that a believer who read his Bible and prayed like he should
would never have any painful emotional problems. This was
taught openly at times, and implied at others. And I believed
what I was taught.

Years later, looking back, I would discover many unresolved
mental health issues in my own life as well as in the lives of other
people in my family. But at that time, I was totally unaware of
them.

My personal decision to follow Christ came during a typical evangelistic invitation given by my pastor following his Sunday evening message. I had just listened to his stirring sermon on the brevity of life and the certainty of judgment.

At the time, I knew I wasn't the world's greatest sinner, but I also knew that many of my activities were contrary to what my church and family had taught me. An additional load of guilt fell on me for involving my girl friend in kinds of entertainment both of us had been taught were wrong.

My resistance to the preacher's appeal broke when my girl friend reached over to return my high school class ring which I had given to her as a token of my love. She told me that until I became a Christian she could no longer go with me.

When that kind of leverage was added to the guilt I felt already, it was enough to send me to the altar. That night I prayed the sinner's prayer. Everyone rejoiced with me because I had given my life to Christ. I still look back on that decision as the wisest in my life, but now I understand that there were many factors in my motivation other than simply responding to the pastor's sermon and yielding to Christ's claims on my life. That decision not only resolved my major conflict with sin, it also relieved tension between me and my family and reconciled me to my girl friend.

To this day, I am unsure which of these factors exerted the most influence on me in making my decision. This is how tightly the spiritual, emotional, and even the social issues of life are intertwined. And more and more, professionals from the fields of both religion and the behavioral sciences are beginning to understand this.

Unhealthy faith—unhealthy feelings

An unhealthy religious experience can be detrimental to your mental health. You can see this in Myrtle's life as I share her story with you. Of course, that's not her real name. Her husband (we'll call him George) became concerned about Myrtle when she came home from a prayer meeting and told him that Jesus was calling her into a special life of prayer.

After that, George began to notice that Myrtle was starting to neglect their home. She had been an immaculate housekeeper. Now, when he came home from work in the evening, the dishes from breakfast were still on the table. The beds weren't made. Their two boys, ages nine and seven, obviously had been allowed to run through the house all day as they pleased.

When George brought these things to Myrtle's attention, she cried and complained that he just didn't understand her. She lamented his lack of spiritual experience. Not long after that, she began sleeping in another bedroom so she wouldn't awaken him when she got up to pray. Of course, that also made it easier for her to avoid what she called the "carnal joy of married love."

George knew something was happening to his wife. But he didn't know what it was or what to do about it. Finally, he talked to the minister in charge of the prayer meeting Myrtle had been attending. The minister agreed that her actions were strange; however, he attributed her behavior to the fact that spiritual experience was a relatively new thing for Myrtle. He encouraged George to be patient and assured him that his wife's rather fanatical emphasis on prayer would soon level off. The minister promised to have a talk with Myrtle.

He talked to her right away but it didn't seem to help. Instead, she took offense at what the minister said. She began to get up even earlier in the morning for her prayer time. George became furious with her when he discovered her waking their sons at five o'clock in the morning to pray with her. When he asked her to explain, she calmly told him Jesus had appeared to her in a vision and told her to include the boys in her early morning prayer because He was calling them to be ministers.

At this point, George made a wise but difficult decision. He sought professional help for Myrtle. At first, she wanted nothing to do with psychiatric help. She decided to come only when her husband convinced her that the people at our center would understand her faith. She agreed to see me.

In the first session I had with Myrtle, she was very anxious to determine whether or not Jesus was real to me. Being assured that He was, she told me about her own encounter with Christ in great detail. Of course, for her it was very real. But it was also a very disintegrative or disabling experience for her.

Healthy faith makes you more effective

A healthy religious experience is *never* disintegrative. It is *never* disabling. In fact, just the opposite is true. It is always integrative. It always enables us to function better in our lives. In Myrtle's case, a healthy religious experience would have helped her function more effectively as a wife, mother, and homemaker. But, to a trained observer, its disintegrative nature marked her spiritual experience as being very unhealthy.

Taking great pains to reinforce the healthy parts of her faith, I assured Myrtle that although her symptoms were religious, her problem was emotional. I asked if she had recently experienced some emotional shock or major personal loss. She confided in me that her father had died recently and her best friend had been killed in a tragic automobile accident about six months prior to the time she came to see me. Myrtle was overwhelmed by these losses. It is impossible for anyone to suffer the deaths of two important people in their world and not be affected in some way.

I suggested to George that the boys be temporarily cared for by another member of the family for a few weeks. Myrtle was hospitalized. During her five-week hospital stay, she was given a combination of medicine, psychotherapy, and rest. Under these conditions and the supervision of our staff psychiatrist, Myrtle made good progress.

After she was released from the hospital, she and George resumed their life together as they had known it before. Gradually, Myrtle regained her ability to take care of two healthy boys and her homemaking chores. I continued to see her for counseling until she had worked through her grief and learned new, healthy ways of applying her faith to her daily life experiences. I helped her learn how to tell the difference between a healthy and an unhealthy religious experience so she didn't need to become afraid of her faith—or fear that the nightmare of her emotional disturbance would return.

Not all forms of Christianity are emotionally healthy. This should come as no surprise to students of the faith. Sick forms of the Christian religion have been around for two thousand years. John writes about the immature believer who is overwhelmed with fear and insecurity (1 John 4:18). Paul writes about a form of Christianity that manipulates and preys on innocent people, and is practiced by "the sleight of men, and cunning craftiness, whereby they lie in wait to deceive" (Ephesians 4:14).

In both of these references, the apostles are dealing with people whose faith has secured them a place in heaven—but they are having a miserable time getting there. When your faith is both biblically sound and emotionally healthy, you will not only make it to heaven; you will also enjoy your trip. You can't beat that combination. Why settle for less?

Now that we've talked about the problem of unhealthy faith, you may be wondering just how to determine whether some of the religious experiences people have are mentally healthy or unhealthy. Is there a way to tell?

If you read the introduction to this book, you noticed I said God is the source of wisdom. As the author of our faith, He has provided in His Word the guidelines we need for keeping it healthy. It is for our benefit to become sufficiently familiar with the Scriptures to know when they are being interpreted in ways contrary to our mental health.

In order to be a good steward of a healthy faith, we need biblical ways of testing religious ideas before we open ourselves to them. Often, in our mass-media world, we are confronted with many sick forms of religion that are made to appear quite appealing. But Paul, in 1 Corinthians 14:29, reminds us how important it is to carefully judge the words of anyone who would try to influence us spiritually. He says, quite bluntly, "Let the prophets speak two or three, and let the other judge."

Ten ways to test your faith

With Paul's words in mind, let's take a look at some practical and biblical guidelines I have defined from my clinical experience for helping us discern the difference between a healthy faith and one that is unhealthy. This kind of mental health insurance is extremely important for Christians. So many of the emotionally troubled people who come to me for help are suffering from symptoms brought on by unhealthy religious experiences or beliefs. Applying these guidelines to your faith can spare you the pain and confusion of an unhealthy faith, and help you to reap all the benefits of a healthy faith.

1. Healthy faith is affirmed in fellowship.

Beware of isolated religious groups that insist on rigid conformity to strange beliefs and practices which have little if any biblical support. Remember, Paul admonished Timothy to display reputable scholarship in his approach to biblical interpretations so that he might "rightly" divide the Word of truth (2 Timothy 2:15). Also, Peter warns the believer ". . . that no prophecy of the scripture is of any private interpretation" (2 Peter 1:20).

Christianity affords us a wide variety of churches which can be identified by their honest differences. These are distinguished from each other by their scholarly interpretations of portions of the Bible. If our faith is healthy, we should be able to identify theologically with at least one of these groups.

When your beliefs are so unique and different that you are unable to find any group of fellow believers with whom you are comfortable, your beliefs are suspect. Remember, Jesus wants His followers to be one with Him and with one another. That is the subject of His priestly prayer as recorded in John 17:21: "That they all may be one; as thou, Father, art in me, and I in thee, that they also may be one in us: that the world may believe that thou hast sent me."

2. Healthy faith sees God as love.

Many believers still struggle with an angry picture of God. They see Him as One whose wrath is to be avoided, rather than as One whose approval is to be gained and whose care for them is constant. We'll take a better look at how this affects a believer's other relationships in Chapter 4 where we discuss, "Anger: Master or Servant?"

Often, believers who view God as angry and wrathful place too strong an emphasis on the Old Testament view of God as an angry judge. It's true that He presided over the flood, the destruction of wickedness in Sodom and Gomorrah, and the expulsion of the Canaanites, but He is also the God and Father of our Lord and Savior Jesus Christ who presided over the birth of His love gift to you and me in Bethlehem.

Each of us has to choose the mental picture of God on which he will focus. Philip was having trouble making the selection, so he said to Jesus, "Lord, show us the Father, and it sufficeth us." And Jesus answered him by saying, "Have I been so long time with you, and yet hast thou not known me, Philip? he that hath seen me hath seen the Father" (John 14:8, 9). When the healthy believer wonders what God is like, he thinks of Jesus.

3. Healthy faith fosters self-esteem.

No other religion in the world places as much value on an individual as does the Christian faith. Of course, the Scriptures insist on us being honest with ourselves about our sins. But God assures us of His love by declaring, "For scarcely for a righteous man will one die: yet peradventure for a good man some would even dare to die. But God commendeth his love toward us, in that, while we were yet sinners, Christ died for us" (Romans 5:7,8).

Isn't it sad to see people focus on their sinfulness rather than on God's love for them? When I focus on my sinfulness, I feel horrible about myself. And yet, I want to be honest about my sins. I can't forget John's reminder that, "If we say that we have no sin, we deceive ourselves, and the truth is not in us." But he also adds, "If we confess our sins, he is faithful and just to forgive us our sins, and to cleanse us from all unrighteousness" (1 John 1:8,9).

Once I have honestly confessed my sins to Jesus, I no

longer want to think about them. Instead, I want to focus on how much God loves me. And how much is that?

Calvary does not tell us how much God loves His children. It reveals God's love for His enemies. Paul puts it this way: "For if, when we were enemies, we were reconciled to God by the death of his Son; much more, being reconciled, we shall be saved by his life" (Romans 5:10).

If you want to know how much God loves you as His child, the next time you see a cross, envision the words "MUCH MORE" written above it in capital letters. Then you have some idea just how much God loves each of His children—including you. That discovery can make a world of difference in the way you view yourself. It also affects the way you feel about God, as we'll see in the next chapter.

4. Healthy faith meets reality.

At any given moment, reality for each of us is a personal combination of past influences, present stresses, and their interactions with each other. These influences and stresses are fourfold in nature: physical, psychological, social, and spiritual.

Such areas of influence and stress tend to impact on each other. For example, in our culture we expect men to be taller than women. Therefore, a man who is genetically determined to be short or a woman who is going to be tall will experience emotional and social stress as a result of this physical factor present in their life.

Being born into poverty or wealth is a social fact of life over which we have no control. However, such an event can have a profound effect on the physical, psychological, and spiritual dimension of one's life.

The sudden loss of wealth, position or a loved one can trigger a functional depression (the kind resulting from situational stress) which drastically affects the physical, social and even the spiritual dimensions of life.

It should be obvious that most of us bring from our past some events and experiences which could adversely affect our mental health. And in addition, all of us must risk

26

stresses from our present which could devastate us. There simply is no life without storms.

In the closing illustration of His Sermon on the Mount, Jesus guarantees the survival of His followers who respond to life's storms as He has taught them—but predicts disaster for those who don't.

> *Therefore whosoever heareth these sayings of mine, and doeth them, I will liken him unto a wise man, which built his house upon a rock: And the rain descended, and the floods came, and the winds blew, and beat upon that house; and it fell not: for it was founded upon a rock. And every one that heareth these sayings of mine, and doeth them not, shall be likened unto a foolish man, which built his house upon the sand: And the rain descended, and the floods came, and the winds blew, and beat upon that house; and it fell: and great was the fall of it.* Matthew 7:24–27

This helps explain why some people are so severely damaged by life, while others survive and even thrive in the face of adversity. At times life deals potentially crippling blows to each of us. But what happens to us is not nearly as critical to our emotional and spiritual health as is the way we choose to react to what happens.

More important to your mental health than influences from your past or stresses from your present are the ways you have learned to talk to yourself about these things. None of us live simply with what we experience in life. We live with the way we choose to feel and think about what we experience. The facts of our experiences are not as critical to our mental health as are the meanings we give them. We teach ourselves a story about the facts of our lives. After we have learned it well, we tell it to ourselves over and over again. The images and feelings these stories create in our minds are what we live with.

27

Solomon wisely observed this when he wrote, "For as he thinketh in his heart, so is he" (Proverbs 23:7). Each of us uniquely perceives his circumstances and responds to them. This accounts for the many different ways people in any given family are affected by the same set of family circumstances even though they share the same home.

In my work as a therapist, I make it very clear to hurting people that no one can change what has happened to them. However, if they are willing to work at it, I can help them find a way of feeling and thinking about what has happened to them that won't hurt so much. Part of this healing is accomplished by a process of creative prayer. The four steps to praying through such a situation are discussed in Chapter 2 and again in Chapter 7. A healthy faith allows you to engage in creative prayer and discover new ways of looking at what has happened to you. It helps you to learn a less destructive version of the painful chapters in your life.

Do you remember the story of Joseph? His brothers envied him and would have killed him had it not been for the chance to sell him into slavery. How do you like that for brotherly love? Once in Egypt, his master's wife had Joseph falsely charged and thrown into prison for not giving in to her seducing ways. Can you imagine how it must have felt to go to jail for doing what was right? There, he was forgotten by his friend—the butler who had promised to remember Joseph when he was restored to Pharaoh's favor. Still, in the face of all this, Joseph refused to become bitter or seek revenge.

In Genesis 50:15–21, Moses preserves this beautiful example of a mentally healthy faith for us:

> *And when Joseph's brethren saw that their father was dead, they said, Joseph will peradventure hate us, and will certainly requite us all the evil which we did unto him. And they sent a messenger unto Joseph, saying, Thy father did command before he died, saying, So shall ye say unto Joseph, Forgive, I pray thee now, the trespass of thy brethren, and their sin; for they did unto thee evil:*

28

and now, we pray thee, forgive the trespass of the servants of the God of thy father. And Joseph wept when they spake unto him. And his brethren also went and fell down before his face; and they said, Behold, we be thy servants. And Joseph said unto them, Fear not: for am I in the place of God? But as for you, ye thought evil against me; but God meant it unto good, to bring to pass, as it is this day, to save much people alive. Now therefore fear ye not; I will nourish you, and your little ones. And he comforted them, and spake kindly unto them.

Joseph had little or no control over what happened to him during those horror-filled years as a slave and prisoner in Egypt. However, he determined to stay in control of how he permitted himself to feel and think about the injustices of those years. He knew that bitterness never hurts those who cause it as much as it does those who harbor it.

5. Healthy faith cushions future shock.

Alvin Toffler, in his book *Future Shock*, explains the mounting levels of stress created by the many interlocking drives and forces of Western man's history. People once were separated by nature's boundaries so that events in one part of the world had little or no effect on those who lived in other parts. Little by little, man's genius for inventing methods of transportation and communication has overcome those boundaries. Today, it is impossible to be sheltered from events in other parts of the world by rivers, mountains, deserts, or oceans. What happens on one part of the planet impacts on the people of every other "civilized" part. Today, we live in a global village.

The pace of change in our society has been picking up speed dramatically since the turn of the century. Ask any senior citizen to describe the changes which have taken place in his or her lifetime. It will amaze you.

They have seen travel go from horse-and-buggy days to lunar landings. They have had to adapt to communication methods that changed from word of mouth and the most primitive of telegraph and telephone systems to the live satellite transmissions of our day. Now, instead of taking weeks, news can be transmitted from any spot on the earth right into people's homes in living color at the moment it is happening. And they have watched as rural communities were swallowed up by sprawling cities and eight-lane superhighways.

One thing about the future which can be predicted with absolute certainty is that the pace of change will continue to accelerate. The wedding of telephone and computer technology is just beginning to make its impact on our communication system. And we have yet to see what supersonic air travel and the space shuttle will do for transportation.

Failure to keep pace with and adapt to these ever-increasing changes results in what Toffler called "future shock." In the face of this rapid acceleration, many believers are struggling with crippling levels of tension, worry, and anxiety. Some are trying desperately to deny the daily realities of their world, rooted to a firm conviction that they must not change in any way.

However, healthy faith helps the believer adapt to change. Some forms of religious orthodoxy are characterized by a style of thinking which is rigid and inflexible. People who hold to this kind of belief are very uncomfortable in the face of change.

Listening to them, you would think that the less a person changes, the more like God he is. In fact, in defense of their position and their refusal to change, these believers often quote Malachi 3:6, "For I am the Lord, I change not," and Hebrews 13:8, "Jesus Christ the same yesterday, and today, and for ever."

I have talked to many Christians victimized by this kind of teaching. I have tried to help them become more flexible in their thinking by helping them realize that since none of us is God or Jesus, we cannot afford the luxury of remaining the same. We must be open to change.

To be sure, there is a healthy fear of any change which would compromise our relationship to Christ. Sometimes our graduate students at EMERGE* experience this kind of fear. They are afraid of the changes that occur as a result of intellectual challenge and self-examination. And they have to be reassured that a healthy faith can accommodate a growing person.

I understand that need because I, too, grew up in a religious environment which taught me to be suspicious of change. I experienced that same kind of anxiety when I was stretching and growing out of some of the unhealthy ideas of my early faith. So, I share with my students a statement God helped me to define for my own reassurance at that time in my life:

> To live is to grow. To grow is to change. If one cannot discern the difference between the change that results from growth and the change that results from the loss of one's faith, his fear of losing his faith makes him resist all change. Then his faith becomes an inhibitor of, rather than a facilitator of, his growth.

Do you know of anything that is living that isn't growing in some way? Do you know of anything that is growing that isn't changing? It is never God's will for our faith to get in the way of our growth. Healthy growth never increases the distance between us and God. In fact, it lessens it. For, the more we learn about life, the greater is our love for Him; the more intense is our desire to know Him.

Unless Saul of Tarsus had been willing to risk growing out of the rigid, inflexible mindset of the Pharisees, he never could have become Paul the apostle to the Gentiles. Before he was converted, he was so legalistic that he said he was "blameless" as far as the law of the Pharisees was concerned (Philippians 3:6). You can't get much more religiously rigid than that!

However, once Christ transformed his mind, Paul became so comfortable with change that he was able to be made "all things to all men, that [he] might by all means

---

* EMERGE is a mental health and learning resource center in Akron, Ohio, founded and directed by Dr. Dobbins.

save some" (1 Corinthians 9:22). More will be said about that transforming miracle in Chapter 5 when we deal with the subject of guilt.

If your faith is healthy, you understand that in the midst of our rapidly changing world there are some things which do not change: God's person, God's Son, and God's Word. Like any good navigator, with your sights on these three fixed points of reference, you can steer your course through any environment and any changes you must face. You can grow through change when your faith is healthy.

6. Healthy faith manages stress and anxiety.

The stress and anxiety of our fast-paced world do not have to be destructive. Dr. Hans Selye, world-renowned specialist on stress, has coined the word "eustress" to describe how the energy created by stress can be converted into productive, creative activities.

Not only is it unrealistic for us to expect to live totally free of stress and anxiety, it is probably impossible. In fact, certain amounts of both stress and anxiety are essential elements in times of excitement, motivation, and growth in life. Think how boring life would be without these moments. A little test anxiety motivates the student to study more, which usually results in a better grade. Entertainers and athletes expect to feel some tension and anxiety just before they go into action. It helps them perform better.

However, large doses of tension and anxiety can cripple a person. Under certain circumstances, the phobic person is literally paralyzed by his anxiety. And I have seen people so overwhelmed by fear that they were unable to leave the security of their home without a family member or friend accompanying them. The fear of doing a less-than-perfect job keeps many obsessive-compulsive men from finishing any of the jobs they start. And a woman suffering from an obsessive fear of dirt or germs may wash her hands fifty to one hundred times a day in an effort to be germ free.

It is difficult to know how many people—including Christians—suffer from these or other forms of psychosomatic illness due largely to an overload of tension and anxiety. It doesn't have to be this way. God's Word abounds with practical solutions to such problems.

As you learn to order your life according to the teachings of Jesus, the tensions and anxieties of life become more manageable. After all, He taught us not to worry about material things, but to put the kingdom of God first in our lives and trust Him to see that our material needs are met (Matthew 6:31–33).

Most of our worries are related to our physical existence. And most of them never materialize. You would think that fact in itself would discourage worrying. And yet, for many it only tends to reinforce worrying. Why? Because they believe in worrying!

If you want to test this, try a little experiment with a group of people. Tell them, "List all of your worries for the past year on a sheet of paper. When you are finished, turn the paper over and list all of the things you worried about which actually happened this past year."

Very few of the things about which they worried actually happened, no doubt. But would that cure the real worriers of worrying? Of course not. They would be wondering how many more things about which they worried would have happened had they not worried about them! Instead of concluding that worrying was a waste of time and energy for them, they would be convinced all the more that worrying really helps.

Worry and fear are notorious thieves of time and energy. In a later chapter I will be suggesting some practical ways for keeping them from stealing your kingdom potential.

When our faith is healthy, we trust more and worry less. God wants us to be good stewards of the things which come into our possession, but none of them are worthy of our anxiety. All of them perish with use. That is why the healthy believer learns to concern himself less with the material things of life and more with life's spiritual matters:

Wherefore if ye be dead with Christ from the rudiments of the world, why, as though living in the world, are ye subject to ordinances, (touch not; taste not; handle not; which all are to perish with the using;) after the commandments and doctrines of men? . . . If ye then be risen with Christ, seek those things which are above, where Christ sitteth on the right hand of God. Set your affection on things above, not on things on the earth.

Colossians 2:20–22; 3:1,2

7. Healthy faith finds joy in giving.

This spiritual principle has to be experienced before one can believe it. "Try it—you'll like it." That's what God's Word is really saying in Malachi 3:10 where we read, "Prove me now herewith, saith the Lord of hosts, if I will not open you the windows of heaven, and pour you out a blessing. . . ."

Giving is contrary to our selfish human nature. We tend to think the greater joy is in receiving. And yet, when parents compare the Christmas memories of having received from their parents with those of giving to their own children, there's no question which memories are more joyful. Seeing the happiness that one's giving brings to those who receive it is the greater joy.

We soon discover that the return on our giving is related to the nature of our giving. The farmer's world is full of examples of this spiritual principle. If we sow sparingly to the soil, the soil returns to us a sparse harvest. However, if we sow liberally to the soil, we reap a liberal harvest.

In giving, we become a part of the people to whom we give. We are represented in whatever their life and ministry become. It is in giving that each of us shares in the harvest of another's life. Once this discovery is made, we no longer give grudgingly or out of necessity. We give from the heart, knowing that "God loveth a cheerful giver" (2 Corinthians 9:7).

8. Healthy faith expresses anger constructively.

No one lives without anger. You may be so threatened by anger that you learn ways of hiding it from yourself;

34

nevertheless, you still experience it. Over a long period of time, hidden anger can be very damaging. If you impulsively act out your anger, you take unnecessary risks which often complicate your life. If you displace your anger—if you express it toward someone you fear less than the person who provoked it—you are likely to damage important relationships in your life.

You are wiser to think of anger as unexpressed energy. This allows you to understand anger management as *energy* management. Finding constructive ways to put that energy to work is the secret of making anger your friend instead of your enemy.

The energy generated by anger can cut grass, scrub floors, drive golf balls, wash walls, and do many other things. Why not put it to work for you? Anger makes a great servant, but a poor master. In Chapter 4, I will share with you the formula we use at our center for helping people put anger to work for them.

9. Healthy faith balances work and play.

Both work and play are important issues in emotional health. The key is balance. Somewhere between "workaholics" and "playboys" there is a blend which is right for you.

Many people are surprised to find out that work is not a part of the curse. When God made man, He gave him a job. Work is essential to health—both physically demanding work (Genesis 2:15; God gave Adam the task of dressing and caring for the Garden of Eden) and intellectual work (Genesis 2:19; God brought the animals to Adam and told him to think of names for them). We need to work with our bodies and our minds.

We spend more time at work than in any other waking activity. This is why it is so important for young people to give careful thought to the kind of work they would find challenging and prepare themselves for it. They should have some definite ideas about their future in the work world by the time they are through junior high school. Without this kind of planning, our young people will allow a major part of their lives to be left to the luck of the job market.

As important as work is, we must also remember that God made man to play. One day in seven He designed for worship, rest, and recreation. We are never to be too saintly to enjoy playing.

When I was a child, the fourth commandment was interpreted to mean, "You can't have any fun on Sunday." There was no play of any kind permitted. I dreaded Sundays. Don't misunderstand me—I believe worship is the most important activity of the Lord's day, but I also believe Sunday is a day for recreation. When this balance is kept, children learn to love worship and adults don't forget how to play.

Remember the importance of play to a healthy life, and keep your sense of humor. This will go a long way toward sparing you the misery of functional depression—the kind of depression that comes when a person is overwhelmed by circumstances in his life. Of course, some kinds of depression are biochemical in nature and have to be treated biochemically. They are not situational in nature. In Chapter 6 you will learn some ways to tell the difference between these two kinds of depression. You will read about my wife's battle with depression and how God helped her overcome it.

10. Healthy faith loves and forgives others.

Paul reminded Timothy, "For God hath not given us the spirit of fear; but of power, and of love, and of a sound mind" (2 Timothy 1:7). Notice that love is the second gift mentioned. Power is the first.

The Greek word for power which Paul used here is *dunamis*. This word refers to miraculous power or, in some instances, to a miracle. In any case, Paul makes it clear to Timothy that God has provided divine enablement for the believer to help him be a loving and forgiving person.

No one can love without the power of love; not even Jesus. He came to love and to lay down His life for His enemies. However, He was only able to do that because He had the power to take up His life again. Remember, Jesus said, "No man taketh [my life] from me, but I lay it down of myself. I have power to lay it down, and I have power to take it again" (John 10:18).

Often, I see believers trying to live the Christian life without any consciousness of God's divine enablement— simply because it is their Christian duty. What a frustrating experience that must be! One of the evidences of being God's child is the expression of a God-given ability to love: "We know that we have passed from death unto life, because we love the brethren. He that loveth not his brother abideth in death" (1 John 3:14).

As you are able to love and forgive, recognize this as God's gift to you. Celebrate it! Express it! And as you do, your ability to love and forgive will expand to include not only your family and friends but also your enemies. Being able to love and forgive your enemies leaves your tomorrows free from the anger, fear and bitterness of your yesterdays.

There's no healthier way to live! There is no healthier way to live than the life Jesus taught. In fact, if there had been a better way to get more out of life, the Bible would have given it to us. It is God's will that His children live life to its fullest. He has given us His Spirit and His Word so that we might know creative living at its best. Several years ago I discovered some secrets in this regard. In the last chapter of this book I'll be sharing them with you.

Remember, even in our crazy, mixed-up world, believers can enjoy the best of mental health. Your faith is an important part of it. Keep it healthy. A healthy faith will enable you to avoid unnecessary mental health risks, support you in the unavoidable storms of life, and help you celebrate it more joyfully when life goes well.

In the following chapter, I want to help you take a close look at your self-image. It is an important part of your mental health. Your faith is a key ingredient in developing and maintaining a healthy self-image, so I will be helping you understand more clearly the relationship between your faith and your self-image.

2

YOU CAN CHANGE YOUR SELF-IMAGE

Jerry and Sue had been seeing me for several weeks. Their marriage was in trouble. Sue resented having to assume so much responsibility for leadership in the family. Whether it was planning their social life, disciplining their three children, or managing the family budget, Sue was the one who was stuck with it. Her way of reacting was to withdraw emotionally from Jerry. Their love life had dwindled to almost nothing. In all their married life, Sue had never been orgasmic.

As you might imagine, in our sessions Sue was the talkative one. However, when Jerry did volunteer a comment I was impressed with his insight and judgment. I remember saying to him, "Jerry, when you do manage to enter into discussion with Sue, your remarks are so helpful. Why don't you talk more?"

Tears filled Jerry's eyes as he replied, "I guess it's because when I was growing up as a kid nobody at home seemed to care what I thought. At our house kids were to be 'seen and not heard' so I've grown up believing it was best to keep my opinions to myself." From that little insight into Jerry's potential, I realized the need to spend some time helping him correct some seriously mistaken ideas about himself which he had accumulated during the early years of his life.

As a result of our time together, Jerry discovered that he wasn't dumb. In fact, he was very bright. He learned how important his opinions were to the success of his marriage and worked hard at developing appropriate ways of expressing them.

Consequently, his behavior in the family changed—rather dramatically. He became more responsive to Sue and more attentive to their children. Sue no longer had to bear the burden of Jerry's passivity. She had always loved him. Now her respect for him began to grow as well. The spark came back into their sex life. With the help of a more assertive partner, Sue became orgasmic.

I can't help wondering how many others—like Jerry—could get much more out of life and contribute much more to their marriages with just a little help in changing the way they see themselves.

There is no biblical guarantee that you will automatically receive healthy feelings about yourself by simply accepting Jesus as your Savior. In fact, many Christians confuse good feelings about themselves with pride and conceit—traits God despises (Proverbs 21:4). These people resist any feelings of healthy self-worth and zealously deplore their worthlessness under the guise of being spiritual. Often, this kind of believer reeks with the odor of spiritual pride.

However, people who truly discover their great worth to God are neither proud nor conceited. In fact, in the process of making this discovery they are humbled by the price of their redemption.

Such a discovery comes only through a sincere application of biblical truth to one's damaged self-image. God's Word gives us many proven prescriptions for achieving and maintaining a healthy self-image. However, prescriptions are powerless to heal unless the medicine is taken according to directions. The truth of Scripture has to be applied if the benefits are to be enjoyed.

What happened to Jerry can happen to any believer who needs to discover his or her new look in Jesus. It can happen to you!

You can change the way you see yourself

The Bible says we are made "in the image of God" (Genesis 1:27). This means that we are "feeling" beings as well as "thinking" beings because this is the kind of being God is. God not only *thinks*—He *feels.* The Scriptures refer frequently to God's thoughts *and feelings.*

As His offspring, you and I experience life through our thoughts *and* our feelings as well. However, we have been taught to pay much more attention to our thoughts than to our feelings. Just stop and think how few opportunities there are for you and me to learn how to live with our *feelings,* compared with the large emphasis, especially in our early school years, on learning how to *think.* When and where are we given a chance to learn about our feelings and how to live with them?

More and more, pastors and church leaders are seeing the tremendous need for us to have a clearer understanding of our feelings and to learn biblical ways of managing them. After all, your stewardship of your feelings affects every relationship in your life. Misunderstandings between mates, friction between parents and children, conflicts among brothers and sisters, hard feelings among people at church—all these tensions in life are aggravated by and often rooted in *feelings.*

People problems come from within

Interpersonal problems usually begin as intrapersonal problems. It has been that way ever since Adam. Do you remember how he explained his disobedience to God? Adam blamed it all on Eve. When God approached Eve on the subject, she was no more inclined to accept responsibility for her behavior than was Adam. She blamed it all on the serpent.

Like Adam and Eve, most of us choose to ignore our responsibility for our problems. They are too painful for us to face. It is much easier and more comfortable for us if we can make other people responsible for what troubles us. If it is not convenient to blame our problems on other human beings, we often blame them on the devil.

According to legend, Martin Luther had a vision in which he saw the devil sitting by the side of the road crying. In the vision, Luther approached the devil and asked him why he was crying. Satan replied, "Because I get blamed for so many things I'm not responsible for!"

Problems *between* people usually begin *within* people. If we were more skilled in identifying and managing problems *within* ourselves, we would have fewer problems *among* ourselves. It is amazing how much brighter the world becomes when we clean our own glasses.

That is why it is so important for you to take a look at the way you feel and think about yourself. Your self-concept colors everything you see in life. It is the lens through which you look at life.

A cartoon I have in my office shows a fellow looking in a mirror. He's asking his reflection a very important question: "Are you *fer* me or *ag'in'* me today?" Very often, your best friend or worst enemy is the person you see when you look in the mirror. If someone were to ask you what you thought of the person *you* see when you look there, what would you say?

How much does Jesus think you are worth?

Here are the questions we're going to be considering during this section on self-worth: What are we referring to when we talk about our self-concept? Why is our self-concept so important? Where do we get our self-concept? If we don't like the one we have, how do we go about changing it?

First, let's take a look at what we are talking about when we refer to self-concept. *Your self-concept consists of what you believe to be important and true about yourself.*

Many people are so anxious and confused that their views of self are very uncertain. They tend to believe whatever the person they are with at the moment says is true about them. If you were to ask them, "What do *you* believe to be honest and true about yourself?" they couldn't tell you.

If you want a practical way of discovering what you believe is true about yourself, why not ask yourself, "How do I feel about the person I'm with when I'm alone?" Or write the following sentence stem ten times and fill in the blanks: "I am a person who _____

_____."

By filling in the blanks, you will discover ten things that you believe to be important and true about yourself. Why not take time to do that now? Then continue with the chapter and find out how these statements color your view of yourself—and of God—and how you believe God sees you.

These statements define the lens through which you look at life. That is why your self-concept is so very important. Everything you experience in life is filtered through it. Even your view of God is filtered through the way you see yourself. In fact, it is difficult—if not impossible—to have a healthy view of God if you do not have a healthy view of yourself. We'll talk more about this a little later.

The secret to being positive can be yours!

Your view of life in general is a product of your self-concept. The more positively you see yourself, the more positive your view of life tends to be. The more negatively you see yourself, the more negative your view of life tends to be. This is part of what Paul refers to in 1 Corinthians 13:12: "Now we see through a glass darkly."

Our fallen nature makes it impossible for us to see life as God intended when He made us in His image. Our limited knowledge and experience further distort our view of life. *Your self-concept will add either clarity or confusion to your view of life. That is why it is so important.*

Where do we get our self-concept? It's obvious that you and I were not born with one. *The view you have of yourself has grown out of the interactions between you and other members of your family during the first three to five years of your life.* It is a product of many things.

Self-image is often affected by the way your parents felt about your arrival. After all, when we come into the world we are very tiny and quite fragile. It is important that the people to whom we are born be pleased with our arrival even if they didn't plan for it. The way they feel about our birth will be communicated to us through subtle nuances of touch, sight, and sound during the times when they feed us, bathe us, and change us.

Many other issues in those preverbal years of your life have an important bearing on your self-concept: How gently or abruptly you were weaned. How patiently or angrily you were toilet-trained. How your parents reacted when they saw you fondle your genitals as an infant. How frequently you were yelled at. How often you were commended. How fairly or unfairly you were disciplined. How much freedom you were given. How much responsibility you were expected to assume.

None of these things should be viewed as solely determining your self-concept. However, any of them may have a more or less important bearing on how a child has learned to feel about himself by the time he is old enough to talk. Remember—no one is born with an image of himself. But by the time he starts to school, he has learned ways of feeling and thinking about himself which tend to be stable over time and highly resistant to change.

Your self-concept is also affected by the number of brothers and sisters you have. How many were already there in the family when you came? How many came after you? Where did you wind up in the parade?

Birth order suggests some general assumptions which may affect a person's self-concept. Not all of these effects are positive. Some couples have been waiting for their first child so they can correct all the parenting mistakes they believe their parents made with them. As a result, a first child is usually the one some parents try to make perfect.

However, a first child has several advantages. He has his parents' full and undivided attention. He does not have to share their love until another child is born. Neither does he have to share his toys. His parents have the time to give him individual attention during those important early months of learning.

On the other hand, greater parental demands are made on the first child than on subsequent children, and parents are often more critical of him. However, he is also likely to receive more parental praise than later children.

As a result of these unique factors, first children tend to be very responsible, highly productive people. After all, they are usually the family's first free babysitter. This may help to explain why some oldest children tend to be a bit bossy as adults. They are also—quite often—extremely conscientious and guilt prone.

The baby of the family usually grows up expecting others to take care of him. It seems that the longer the family has been without a baby before this one is born, the more the family members tend to cater to this baby. Parents should realize the need to provide this kind of child with plenty of experiences with other children his age, to make up for the absence of children close to his age at home. This will help him be less self-centered and better able to share with others. Because of all the love and attention that he is likely to receive, the baby of the family is seldom insecure.

Children raised in the middle positions of a large family are the ones most likely to suffer from low self-esteem. They are not close enough to the front of the line to get the love they need, and they are not close enough to the back of the line to have been the baby very long.

Of course, birth order is just one of many variables that make up the matrix of one's self-concept. Its ultimate influence is determined by each child's reaction to his place in the family. Therefore, the most critical factor involved in the role that birth order plays is not the position itself, but how one perceives it. This perception flows out of the parent-child relationship.

So, if you can remember having healthy thoughts and feelings about yourself as a child, thank God for your parents. And if your parents are still alive, thank them. There is no more valuable gift a parent can give a child than that of a healthy understanding of who he is and who God is.

Your self-concept is your key to happiness

Your happiness is largely determined by how you feel and think about yourself and how you choose to feel and think about what happens to you in life. Both of these affect and are affected by the lens through which you look at life—your self-concept. Solomon said it well: "As he thinketh in his heart, so is he" (Proverbs 23:7).

Jesus expanded on this important truth in Matthew 12:34,35: ". . . For out of the abundance of the heart the mouth speaketh. A good man out of the good treasure of the heart bringeth forth good things: and an evil man out of the evil treasure bringeth forth evil things." What do these verses mean? Here Jesus explains that you can know something of the content of a person's heart from listening to his conversation. This is a basic tenet of psychology.

When you listen to a person talk, he tells you what is in his heart. Whatever he has stored in his heart he can't forever keep still about. Sooner or later, if there is an abundance of it in his heart, it will surface in his conversation.

I encourage you to begin to listen to what you say when you talk to others. What are your favorite topics of conversation? How broadly conversant are you with the issues of the day? Is there depth to your conversation or do you major in trivia? When you talk about people do you generally tend to build them up or do you tear them down? As you analyze your philosophy of life from your conversation, is it optimistic or pessimistic?

How do you talk to yourself?

As important as it is for you to be aware of your conversation with others, it is even more important to tune in to what you say when you talk to yourself. What you choose to say to other people is just a sample of what you choose to say when you talk to yourself. The way you talk to yourself grows out of and contributes to your self-concept.

For example, if you have grown up with the idea that other people are smarter than you are and stronger than you are, then you are likely to feel inferior and insecure much of the time. This view of yourself is going to be reflected in your internal speech patterns (how you talk to yourself) and in your conversation with others.

It is from the way you choose to talk to yourself that your happiness or unhappiness flows. I've had people tell me, "But you just don't know what it was like in my family when I was growing up." I usually respond with, "What has happened to you in life is not nearly as important to your happiness as is the way you are choosing to *respond to* what has happened to you."

After all, none of us lives with just the facts of his life. We

45

live with the story we tell ourselves about the facts of our lives.

None of us grow up in ideal circumstances. One of the big deceptions of our fallen minds is the belief that if we had another person's circumstances we would be happier. However, even if we had someone else's circumstances, we would still interpret them in our own way.

As an example, let me tell you a story I once heard about a duck hunter who bought a dog to retrieve his game for him. The first time he took the dog hunting no one else was with him. On his first shot, a duck fell into the water. Immediately, the dog walked out *on* the water, picked up the game in his mouth, and returned it to his master.

The man couldn't believe his own eyes. However, the same thing happened three more times before the day was over. As he stowed his game and his gear in the van, he thought to himself, "I could never tell anybody about this. No one would believe me. They'd think I was crazy." So he decided he would take a hunting buddy with him the next time. He did.

The day went like it had gone when he was alone. Every time he or his buddy would shoot a duck his dog would walk out *on* the water, pick it up, and bring it back to them. The friend gave no indication that he noticed anything different about the dog. Finally, they packed their game and gear back into the van. The dog's proud owner couldn't tolerate his friend's silence any longer. He turned to his friend and asked, "Did you notice anything unusual about my dog today?"

"Yeah," his friend replied. "He can't swim, can he?"

You view your own circumstances and those of others in your own way. Circumstances don't determine your happiness. It is the way you choose to view them and talk to yourself about them which becomes critical to your happiness.

A person with a negative self-image can be in the most positive circumstances possible and not find anything to be encouraged about. On the other hand, a person with a positive self-image can weather some very severe storms in life without being done in by them.

People who don't know me have often said to me, "You can say all that about interpreting your circumstances positively because life has been kinder to you than it has to me. If you knew the difficult circumstances in which I grew up, you'd know why I feel like I do."

I suppose it's easy for us to assume that life has treated other people better than it has us, especially if we don't know them. So let me tell you something about my early life.

My mother was married the first time when she was fifteen. Her husband brutalized her, so she divorced him. When she was eighteen, she married my father. When she was nineteen, they were expecting me. Thirteen days after she gave birth to me, she died. My birth killed my mother.

My aunt had been married and was left a widow with a little girl. So, when my father needed somebody to take care of me and she needed help in taking care of her little girl, the two of them got married. Six years later, they had a girl of their own. I grew up in a home where it was, "your kid, my kid, and our kid."

This is just a little peek into the pages of my life, but I hope it helps you see that pain and trouble come to everyone. If we don't remind ourselves of this fact, it becomes easy to think that we're the only ones whom life hurts. Life pains everyone. But it's how you choose to talk to yourself during these storms that determines to a great extent how they will affect you.

You may ask, "Why is the way I talk to myself so important?" Because no other person can talk to you as fast as you talk to yourself. A minister or public speaker can only talk to you at the rate of about two hundred to three hundred words per minute. But your mind is so amazing that it allows you to talk to yourself in thought at speeds of three thousand to four thousand words per minute. This is why it is so easy for your thoughts to stray sometimes during a church service. If a speaker can get your attention, your mind will stay with what that person is saying. But if he gets a little boring, your mind will take you on a dozen side trips into your yesterdays or your tomorrows.

Remember, others can only talk to you at the rate of two hundred to three hundred words per minute. Your parents cannot talk to you any faster than that. Neither can a friend or your mate. This is why I advise anyone who is married to a person who is miserable *not* to try to make that person happy. Trying to make a miserable person happy is a good way to lose your own happiness. Remember, for every hundred words you can use to bring your mate out of his misery, his own internal speech habits will have presented him with a thousand words to convince him that life is still as miserable as he thinks it is. You're outnumbered ten words to one before you start. You may as well save your breath to cool your soup.

Only you can change your feelings

God knows that your happiness and mine is too important an issue for Him to put in anyone's hands but yours or mine—and His. It is unfair for any of us to expect someone else to change the way we feel about ourself and life. Nor do I want anyone else determining whether I'm going to be happy. I want that freedom and responsibility right in my own grasp and God's.

If in the process of growing up in your home you received a wholesome self-concept through which to view life, then you have no need to change your self-image. However, many of us were born to parents preoccupied with their own pain at the time we came into their lives. They were unaware of how we were learning to feel and think about ourselves as we were growing up with them. They wouldn't have intentionally given us a negative way of looking at life, or a miserable way of seeing ourselves, for anything in the world. But our arrival came when they were so preoccupied with hurts from their past and pressures from their present that they didn't understand how we were learning to look at life. Provision for our emotional comfort was lost in concern over their own pain.

Can a believer who has a damaged self-image change the way he feels and thinks about himself? Yes, thank God, he can. This is what being born again is all about.

Paul tells us that we can all be changed more and more into the image of Christ (2 Corinthians 3:17, 18). As we receive our natural self-image from the parents to whom we are born naturally, we have an opportunity, once we have been regenerated, to be recreated in the image of our heavenly Father.

Regeneration makes *recreation* *possible,* but not *inevitable.*

Once a person is born again he has the opportunity of becoming the person God knows he can be in Jesus (John 1:12). What he does with this opportunity is left to his own initiative.

For many of us, achieving this goal requires the transformation of the badly damaged self-image we bring with us into God's kingdom. The directions of God's Word and the dynamics of His Spirit are at our disposal in our pursuit of this goal. However, we have to apply these resources if our view of ourself is going to be changed.

How can you go about changing your self-concept?

Many believers expect this to happen magically at the instant of conversion, with little or no personal involvement. Although the miracle of God's grace is an essential dynamic in any such transformation, it also requires the believer to put forth conscious and deliberate effort in the process. *God doesn't require you to do what you can't, but He does expect you to do what you can.* Here are some practical steps you can take in changing your self-concept.

1. See yourself as a lovable person.

This will be something new for some. It's amazing to see how many of God's people find it difficult to think of themselves as lovable. It is even difficult for some to receive a compliment. How easy is it for you to accept a compliment? When someone says to you, "Oh, you look so nice tonight," do you find it necessary to tell them you bought your dress on sale or got your suit at a discount? Are you likely to respond to a compliment with an apology? Is it difficult for you to simply say, "Thank you, I appreciate that"?

How easy is it for you to receive expressions of love from other people? Can you see why they would love you? Do you see yourself as a lovable person?

Your heavenly Father wants you to see yourself this way. Regardless of how you may feel about the way your earthly parents viewed you, when you look at the Cross there can never be any doubt about how your heavenly Father feels about you. Remember, if you're God's child, Calvary does not tell you how much God loves you. Calvary only tells you how much God loves His enemies. Romans 5:6–8 says, "For when we were yet without strength, in due time Christ died for the ungodly. For scarcely for a righteous man will one die: yet peradventure for a good man some would even dare to die. But God commendeth his love toward us, in that, while we were yet sinners, Christ died for us."

"Well," you may say, "if God loves His enemies that much, then how much does He love His children?" Perhaps you will only begin to understand how much God loves you as His child when you write above the cross the words, "Much more." Romans 5:9,10 tells us, *"Much more* then, being now justified by his blood, we shall be saved from wrath through him. For if, when we were enemies, we were reconciled to God by the death of his Son, much more, being reconciled, we shall be saved by his life" (italics added).

If you want to remember how much God loves you as His child, I would suggest that you make a cross somewhere in the flyleaf of your Bible. Above that cross write the question, "How much does God love me?" Then arch over the cross the words, "Much more!"

Can you fathom that? You and I are that lovable in God's sight. That's the way your heavenly Father wants you to see yourself. He wants you to know how lovable you are.

2. Realize how valuable you are to God.

One of the common afflictions I see believers suffering from is a very low sense of self-worth. Many believers simply do not understand the difference between being *unworthy* and being *worthless.* They make a mental equation of the two words. To them, unworthy = worthless.

These terms are *not* synonymous. To be unworthy is not equal to being worthless. None of us can ever be worthy of the price our heavenly Father paid for us. How could we ever be proud enough to think of ourselves as deserving of the blood of Christ? However, if we hadn't been worth it to our heavenly Father, He would never have paid such a price for us.

Worth is established by the amount one is willing to pay for what is being offered for sale. It is a value that is really set in the marketplace. When you and I were sold under sin, our heavenly Father redeemed us, not with corruptible things such as silver or gold, but with the precious blood of Christ. "For God so loved the world, that he gave his only begotten Son, that whosoever believeth in him should not perish, but have everlasting life" (John 3:16). And, "Forasmuch as ye know that ye were not redeemed with corruptible things, as silver and gold, from your vain conversation [way of life] received by tradition from your fathers; but with the precious blood of Christ, as of a lamb without blemish and without spot" (1 Peter 1:18,19).

I can never be worthy of that price. You can never be worthy of that price. But the fact that Christ paid it makes me know I'm not worthless. Nor are you. You and I are of great worth to God.

Jesus said each human being is worth more than the total of all the material wealth in the whole world. Look at what He said as recorded in Mark 8:36: "For what shall it profit a man, if he shall gain the whole world, and lose his own soul?" Were it possible for one man to pursue and possess the wealth of the whole world, and were he to lose himself in the process, Jesus declares that what he would lose (himself) is worth more than what he would gain in material possessions.

You may be thinking, *But I remember a Scripture that says when we've done everything we ought to do, we should consider ourselves unprofitable servants (see* Luke 17:10). That's true—unprofitable, but not worthless. Remember that profit is also an economic term. It refers to the amount returned to the investor in excess of the amount of his investment.

How can you and I return to God an amount in excess of the price He paid for our redemption? If I were to do everything that I could possibly do to repay my heavenly Father for the price of my redemption, I still would have to consider myself unprofitable.

Jesus did not tell that parable to make us feel worthless. He simply wants us to know that when our heavenly Father sent Him to pay the price of our redemption it was no business deal. It was a love affair. And love never looks for profit. To your heavenly Father you are a lovable person. He also considers you to be a valuable person. You are lovable and valuable. Begin to say that to yourself over and over again.

3. Think of yourself as a forgivable person.

Many believers suffer the needless pain of unhealthy guilt, unconsciously assuming that there is some virtue in continuing to suffer for their own sins. Friend, it was Christ's sufferings which atoned for our sins, not our own. And when He suffered, He not only suffered enough for my sins and your sins, He suffered enough for the sins of the whole world. So there is no virtue to be gained in anyone's continuing to suffer for his own sins. Jesus suffered enough.

You may have to live with the natural consequences of some previous sin. But it is never God's will for you to continue to suffer guilt for that sin. For example, a person may drive his automobile under the influence of alcohol and lose a limb in an accident. He never will regain his limb, but God doesn't want him to suffer additionally crippling guilt the rest of his life.

There is no sin you can confess that God won't forgive. Satan, as the accuser of the believer, puts condemning thoughts into our minds. He may suggest that what you did at some point in your past is too wicked for even God to forgive. But remember, he's a liar. God's Word says that "If we confess our sins, he is faithful and just to forgive us our sins, and to cleanse us from all unrighteousness" (1 John 1:9).

Anything I am honest enough to confess, God is faithful

enough to forgive. If you have confessed it to Christ, He has forgiven it. Now, practice saying to yourself, "I am a forgivable person." Say that to yourself over and over again until every bit of guilt from your past is gone . . . under the blood of Christ . . . in the past . . . never to be remembered against you again. "I, even I, am he that blotteth out thy transgressions . . . and will not remember thy sins." That's how Isaiah recorded this truth (Isaiah 43:25).

4. See yourself as a changeable person.

At times, the process of change may require us to pray through some of our old hurts. This form of creative prayer is a simple self-help technique I have discovered to be effective in my own life and have used to help many others achieve desired changes.

I have already shared with you the fact that my birth killed my mother. As I grew up, the way I interpreted that fact changed several times. When I was four, I wondered why I couldn't have had a mommy out of whose "tummy" I came. As an ornery ten- or eleven-year-old kid, I was putting those facts together to say, "The reason I get into so much trouble is that I'm a bad kid. After all, my birth killed my mother."

As a teenager, after I became a Christian, I became more and more aware of an increasing desire to go to my mother's grave. I hadn't been there in years. The first few times I went, I wept to think that a nineteen-year-old young woman had died to give me life, but I still left with that hurt in me. Then on one particular visit when I was nineteen years old, as I stood there thinking about how young my mother had been when she died, the Holy Spirit inspired this thought in my mind: "Not only did Jesus die for you but your mother died for you. How valuable your life must be. See that you make it count for something."

My mother's death was still the result of my birth. I couldn't change the facts. But now I was saying that somehow her death added to the worth of my life. I needed to make my life count for something. I had changed the way I put the facts together. God had helped me discover a less painful way of talking to myself about the facts of my life.

What He did for me I have seen Him do for many others. Your self-image can be changed by changing the way you put together certain painful parts of your past. Even though you can't change the facts, you can change your interpretation of them with God's help.

I see many people discover those creative changes in their view of life's hurts through creative prayer. Since people sometimes express intense feelings which might be frightening to others or misunderstood, I encourage them to practice creative prayer when they are alone. Here are the four steps in the process:

1. *Talk to God honestly about what hurts you.*

Great men and women of Scripture have always found the courage to do this, and so can you. It isn't easy, but it is the only way prayer can bring you the practical help you need when life is hurting you.

Look at the way Jacob resolved the issues of guilt and fear he carried for years against Esau. He was a whole night in prayer coming to terms with those feelings (Genesis 32). Remember David's honesty when he bared his heart to God over what went on between him and Bathsheba (Psalm 51). And don't forget the bitter tears Peter shed over his denial of Christ (Matthew 26:75).

Whatever the issues may be in your life that are keeping you from seeing yourself the way God sees you in Christ, determine to talk to God honestly about them.

2. *Express your feelings about your hurts to God.*

Usually, as you begin to talk honestly to God about what hurts you, you will find the feelings associated with those hurts surfacing. Express those feelings. You may want to weep. You may find yourself expressing intensely angry feelings to God. David did. In Psalm 58:6 he begs God to break the teeth of his enemies. In Psalm 59:13–15 he prays concerning his enemies, "Consume them in wrath, consume them, that they may not be: and let them know that God ruleth in Jacob unto the ends of the earth . . . And at evening let them return: and let them make a noise like a dog, and go round about the city. Let them wander up and down for meat. . . ."

You may be thinking, "But I don't want God to know I feel that way about my enemies." Now, think how ridiculous that is! If those feelings are there, how can you hide them from God? You need to get those feelings out in the presence of someone who will keep them confidential and someone you can trust. Even though you would never act out those feelings, carrying them around buried inside of you can keep you from enjoying life. You need to express them to God.

As you pour your feelings out to God in a time of private prayer, you will reach a time when you have really bared your soul. Everything bottled up inside you has been emptied out before the Lord. The burden of your heart has lifted. You are now ready for step three.

3. *Meditate for a new meaning from your old hurts.*

You can never *think* differently about your old hurts until you *feel* differently about them. Remember what we said earlier: you experience life in your *feelings and* your *thoughts.* However, once you've emptied out your old feelings before God you are in a position for Him to comfort you in your thoughts and show you a new way of looking at your old hurts.

Just as God helped David turn loose of his hatred and bitterness toward those who had hurt him, the Lord will help you surrender your hurts and will suggest to your thoughts new and more constructive ways of looking at them as you quietly meditate before Him.

Remember David's prayer, "Search me, O God, and know my heart: try me, and know my thoughts: and see if there be any wicked way in me, and lead me in the way everlasting" (Psalm 139:23,24).

4. *Praise God for the new meaning He gives you!*

As God gives you the ability to see your old hurt in a new and less painful way, thank Him and praise Him for it. Repeat the new meaning several times in praise and prayer so that when in the future Satan suggests the old meaning in your thoughts again you will have learned the new one so well and will have embedded it so deeply in your mind that the old one will have no more grip on you.

Don't expect all of this to happen in just one session of creative prayer. It may, but it is more likely to require several sessions to bring the needed healing in most cases. After all, we didn't get the way we are in minutes, and we're not likely to become completely different in just minutes. We have become the way we are through a process. And, most likely it will require a process to change us. But that process has to start sometime and someplace in your life. Why not let it be now?

It doesn't make any difference how old you are. Your future can be different from and better than your past. Look at Grandma Moses. She was past retirement age before she discovered her genius for painting. And Colonel Sanders was old enough to live on Social Security before he became a millionaire.

You don't have to stay the way you are. Each of us has within him an undiscovered world of divine potential. Jesus wants to put you in touch with that. You can know exciting change in Him.

God doesn't want you to continue to be crippled by the pain of your past. He has more wholesome ways for you to view these things. And, He wants you to be able to see yourself as He sees you—lovable, valuable, forgivable, and changeable.

The next time you look in a mirror I want you to say, "I'm looking at someone God loves. I'm looking at someone God says is valuable. I'm looking at someone who has been totally forgiven. I'm looking at someone who is becoming more and more like the heavenly Father."

When we begin to see ourselves as God sees us in Jesus, then the world begins to see Jesus in us. Then, we are well on our way to defeating self-consciousness and fears which cripple so many believers. In our next chapter, we will be taking a closer look at some practical ways of dealing with these would-be giants who threaten to keep us from our Promised Land.

3

Nothing to Fear But Fear Itself

Each of us knows what it is to be afraid. No human being lives totally free from fear. In fact, there is probably an inverse relationship between bravado and real courage. The braver a person claims to be, the more likely he is to be suffering from fear. The Apostle John records what we all have discovered by experience, "Fear hath torment" (1 John 4:18).

I vividly recall the fear that gripped me in the middle of the night several years ago. I had awakened, looked out the upstairs bedroom window, and seen someone who was apparently trying to steal our car. I was so frightened by what I saw that when I called the police to report the attempted theft I began to whisper to them over the phone. The man who was taking the information had to assure me that if I would keep the lights off in the house it was perfectly safe to talk loud enough to be heard over the phone. Only then was I able to speak up so that he could hear me.

Fear tends to paralyze

The torment that accompanies fear tends to paralyze us. Often when it strikes we cannot think clearly or act wisely. Undoubtedly, this is one of the reasons Jesus repeatedly encouraged His disciples not to be afraid. Fear blinds us to alternatives in problem-solving and options for decision-making which would otherwise be obvious to us. As we learn to become aware of the Lord's presence in our daily lives, we trust Him more in times when we are afraid and draw from that awareness the courage to respond to life in wiser, more creative ways. Sometimes life confronts us with the need for this kind of mature trust in God before we have had time or opportunity to develop it.

Recently, I sat with a pregnant teenager. She and the teenage young man involved in the pregnancy with her had met at church. She was a believer, but he made no profession of faith. They had gone together for several months. He had convinced her that he loved her dearly and wanted to marry her. However, after she told him she was pregnant there were several weeks when his anger and resentment toward her were so intense that he rejected her altogether. He wouldn't even talk to her over the phone.

By the time she talked to me she had already seen her pastor who had helped her confess her sexual misbehavior to the Lord. She had found the forgiveness she needed in dealing with the overwhelming guilt of such a situation. As a believer, she had found the courage to resist the pressure her boyfriend and his family had put on her to have an abortion.

When she saw me she was struggling with the remaining options. None of them seemed to be good ones. She was trying to determine which of them would be the least destructive. Should she place the baby for adoption through a Christian child placement agency? If so, would the adoptive parents be able to give the baby as much love and opportunity as she could? Would they be able to offer more? What effect would being adopted have on the child's future? How could she live knowing she had a child growing up in someone else's home?

Should she keep the baby and raise it by herself? Her parents would help her, but she would have to bear the primary responsibility. Could she count on regular support payments from the child's natural father? Could she live on what she could get from welfare? How fair was it to expect her parents to meet the expenses of this child out of their limited budget? What kind of opportunities could she give this child as a single parent? Would any other man want to marry her if she brought this child into the marriage?

Should she marry the child's father? He has told her he will marry her, but he doesn't want to until after the baby is born. What if she does marry him? He's not a believer. How long could the marriage be expected to last? Having suffered the rejection, embarrassment, and guilt of being single and pregnant, must she also assume the high risk of being divorced and a single parent before she is thirty?

What are the chances that this teenager, or any other teenager for that matter, can overcome the fear and anxiety of such a moment to adequately consider questions like these? It is extremely difficult for any person, regardless of her age, to see the wisest option for her in such a pressure-packed situation. Even if this young woman can see her wisest option, what are the chances she will find the courage to act on it?

This kind of insight and courage can only come to us in life's frightening and anxious moments when we are willing to focus on God's presence with us and His will for us.

After having thoroughly discussed each of these options with this young lady, I said, "I can certainly understand why you are overwhelmed by fear and anxiety. Any normal person in your situation would be. That someone so young should have to make such an awesome decision is regrettable. However, you are a Christian. And God knows the wisest way for you at this crossroads in your life. Even though your situation has resulted from your own misbehavior and carelessness, don't add to your pain by assuming God has forsaken you. He hasn't. If you will open yourself to an awareness of His presence in your mind and spirit He will help you discern which of the remaining options is best for you. You can trust Him to guide you in the days ahead. It is important for you to be willing to move in any of these directions. Only then can you trust your final decision to represent God's wisdom for your situation."

In my prayer with her, I asked God to make His presence real to her in that frightening time of her life. I asked Him to help her rise above the pressure of the moment and her own desires. I prayed that in the days that followed she would be willing to consider any one of the remaining options which consistently and persistently seemed to surface in her mind as representing God's guidance for her.

As she left my office, she thanked me for making her aware of the ways in which her fear and anxiety could blind her. She expressed appreciation to me for helping her define and think through each of the options facing her. She assured me that she never was more aware of her need of the Lord, and expressed a determination to find and do His will.

I hope she does. As undesirable as this situation may be, at least it brought to her an awareness of God's unfailing love and how He can rescue her from anxiety and fear. It is unfortunate to have to face such a severe crisis so early in life, but if this young woman can learn to trust the Lord in such a frightening moment, she has gained a lesson in crisis management which will serve her well in the future.

On the other hand, through the years I have seen many men and women whose lives have been paralyzed by fears which were not so easily understood. It's one thing to be frightened of circumstances which would scare anyone. It is another thing for your life to be paralyzed by irrational fears.

For example, some people are so fearful of germs that they are gripped by an overwhelming compulsion to wash their hands. Of course, I'm not talking about the normal needs for cleanliness we were all taught as children. This kind of compulsion even goes far beyond the scrupulous actions of a person who is extremely particular about personal cleanliness. It is not unusual for a person who is phobic of germs to wash his or her hands a hundred times a day or more. Obviously, they are crippled by their exaggerated fear of germs and dirt.

Other people are so fearful of social situations they cannot leave their homes by themselves. They are literally prisoners in their own homes. They cannot work steadily. If such a person is married, his mate is often seriously neglected because of this fear.

Such fear may seem ridiculous to others, but it is very real to the sufferer. Without competent professional help these people are likely to remain victims of fear for many years. Even with the best of professional help, recovery may be slow and difficult.

This is why it is important to see unhealthy fear as a devastating enemy early in life. Almost always, if unhealthy fear can be identified early, it can be conquered.

The believer can find in his faith some very practical ways of dealing with unhealthy fear. Later in this chapter you will be introduced to some of them. You will learn where fear comes from, some ways of telling the difference between healthy and unhealthy fear, and some effective ways of defeating fear.

Where does fear come from?

We haven't always been afraid. Before we were born we had a fear-free environment. Life is never more comfortable or secure than during those last few weeks inside mother. Just think of what it must have been like. Absolutely no worries! Mother's body took care of everything.

Before birth there is no concern about food. Mother's body takes care of that. There is no need to breathe. Mother's body takes care of that, too. Even elimination takes place automatically. In fact, nestled in the womb, comforted by the sound of mother's heartbeat, amniotic fluid even provides us our own private water bed. Can you imagine what a shock it is when the plug is pulled and birth begins?

This is our introduction to fear. Suddenly and without warning we are shocked into the world outside mother! Now we have to find our own oxygen. For the first time, we are hungry. And for the first time, mother has to change the diaper!

Obviously, anxiety and fear begin at birth. Thomas Hobbes was right when he said, "Myself and fear were born twins."

Babies have to learn to be comfortable with movement. Every baby is afraid of falling. After all, before birth mother's body was always there for support. However, if you hold a baby in your arms and suddenly let go you can see his startled reflex.

Babies also fear abandonment. Viewing birth through a baby's eyes, it isn't hard to understand this fear. Several weeks before birth the fetus tunes in to the world of sound within his mother—fluid sounds and, most important, mother's heartbeat. The birth process forces the fetus out of his mother's body with very little notice. Then, he is no longer close enough to hear her familiar and reassuring heartbeat.

As you can see, we have a long history with fear. It is the first emotion we learn to experience. Before we had any fixed ideas about ourselves, we knew what it was to be afraid.

Healthy vs. unhealthy fear

What's the difference between healthy and unhealthy fear? We all know that fear is painful. However, some people have to be taught that fear can cause pain. They know what physical pain is, but have denied the emotional pain that fear can bring.

Undoubtedly, the teenager I told you about earlier in this chapter will never experience more pain than she was then experiencing. Even though the physical pain of giving birth is intense, it could not compare with her emotional pain. And, although her emotional pain was great, I had to help her identify it before she could experience it and cope with it. It is important to know when you are hurting emotionally.

Remember, pain can be our friend. It warns us of danger. If we never experienced pain we would never recognize danger. Without the pain of healthy fear we couldn't survive. So let's thank God we can be afraid!

Healthy fear warns us of danger. It warns us of the painful consequences of disobedience. I don't know how your parents dealt with your disobedience, and I certainly don't believe every child has to be spanked. But that's the only language some of us ever understood. I was "reared." And, sometimes I can still feel it in my memories.

Fear of the consequences of disobedience also teaches us not to break the law. Healthy fear teaches us healthy limits. This makes our behavior predictable and orderly society possible.

Holy fear

The most important of our healthy fears is fear of the Lord. Solomon says this is the beginning of wisdom (Proverbs 9:10).

Unfortunately, many people confuse being afraid of God with the fear of the Lord. If someone is afraid of God he has had to learn that fear.

How does a person learn to be afraid of God? Sometimes frustrated and impatient parents threaten disobedient children with God's judgment. Or, an overzealous evangelist may try to scare people into becoming Christians. However, neither of these approaches to people produces anything even remotely similar to what Solomon defines as "the fear of the Lord." These experiences are more accurately understood as a fear of parents or a fear of preachers. No parent or preacher can put "the fear of the Lord" in you—nor do most of them want to.

You learn "the fear of the Lord" when you first experience His presence. What makes this experience the beginning of wisdom? You never forget it. You are left with an overwhelming sense of awe and wonder. A reverence for God is forged in your mind. Continuing to experience His presence helps you order the priorities of your life more wisely. Material concerns become less important than spiritual ones.

"The fear of the Lord" does not strike terror to our hearts. It gives birth to wisdom in our minds. It puts a different perspective on other things we tend to call important. It gives us a different way to calculate what pleasure is and helps us choose more wisely how we will spend our time and energy.

Many believers are dominated by another kind of fear. It's not awe. It's not wonder. It's not reverence. It's terror! They see God suspending them over hell by a thread. They fear the return of Christ. They fear "the mark of the beast." They fear the tribulation. They fear death.

Some even fear they have committed a sin God considers unpardonable. People who fear they have committed the unpardonable sin are pathetic. Among the hundreds of people I have seen for counseling, I have never found one whose sins were unpardonable. It is never God's will for people to suffer this kind of misery. However, because this problem is the source of so much torment for so many people, I deal with it in detail in Chapter 5.

Why are you a Christian?

Some people are Christians because they love God and enjoy being Christians. Other people are Christians because they are afraid not to be. Have you met people like that? God does not want you to serve Him because you are afraid of Him. He wants you to serve Him because you love Him. John says it this way: "There is no fear in love; but perfect love casteth out fear: because fear hath torment. He that feareth is not made perfect in love. We love him, because he first loved us" (1 John 4:18,19).

A healthy faith should help you get the most out of life. I have never been able to understand this distorted idea of the Christian life being dull, drab, and uninteresting. Frequently, I run into someone who implies that you can't have fun and be a Christian. I enjoy watching the look on such a person's face when I challenge them to show me one thing that is good for me as a human being that I can't enjoy as a Christian.

It is God's will for me to take good care of my mind and body, but His Word forbids me nothing that is consistent with my health and wholeness. As Jesus reminds us, it is the thief who comes to steal, to kill, and to destroy. God's presence opens to us a more abundant way of life (John 10:10).

How to conquer unhealthy fear

Often when we are small our fears are related to our physical survival. Do you remember any of your early childhood fears? I do. I can remember lying on my bed at night watching the shadow of tree limbs mirrored on my bedroom wall as they swayed in the wind. Until I was old enough to know what I was seeing, I would imagine those shadows were all kinds of ghosts coming to get me.

Most parents have to help their small children through such painful periods of irrational fear. Often such fears surface at night. The wise parent will keep a light on in the child's bedroom. Even this may not be enough to provide the comfort he needs. For a few nights, it may be necessary for a parent to stay in the child's bedroom with him until he goes to sleep. The light plus the reassuring presence of mom or dad should help the child conquer his fear. Within a few nights, the light alone will be all the child needs. Later, he will develop the courage to turn the light off and go to sleep on his own.

Fear of the dark, fear of snakes, fear of spiders—these are only a few of the many specific fears of children. Through our parents' love we grow out of most of our specific fears by the time we are eight or nine years old. However, most of us come into adult life a little phobic about some things.

Some people don't like to ride elevators. They suffer intense anxiety when they are confined in small spaces. This reaction is known as claustrophobia. It's interesting to watch what people do on elevators. Many are so uncomfortable they seldom look at others. They look at the ceiling. They look at the floor. They look at the wall.

Then, there's acrophobia—fear of high places. Once in a while, I have a little bout with that when I get on high places. I get curious about what it might feel like to jump. That feeling so frightens me that I move back from the edge or railing. This gives me a little taste of what it must be like for people who suffer crippling phobias.

Until they are faced, unhealthy fears will never be conquered. As adults, most of us have very few specific fears. Our fear is more general in nature. It is more anxiety-provoking than frightening. We fear talking in front of people. We fear meeting new people. We fear failing. We fear rejection.

Many of these are related to self-consciousness. Often, Christians find self-consciousness a major source of anxiety. Later in the chapter I will be offering some practical help for people suffering from this fear. Right now, I'm going to give you four ways to deal with unhealthy fear and anxiety.

1. You can control anxiety.

First of all, learn some simple, physical controls for anxiety. Start with deep-breathing exercises. God gave you lungs for specific purposes. Sighs and deep breaths are not simply unconscious reactions to life stress. They are nature's ways of relieving you of anxiety for a moment.

When doing deep-breathing exercises, sit with your back against some support. Put your feet as flat on the floor as you can. Put one hand on your diaphragm. Put your other hand on top of it so you can feel yourself inhale and exhale. Then, slowly breathe in as much air as you can. Now, slowly breathe out as far as you can. Do this three times. Breathe in, and out.

After you have inhaled and exhaled three times, just close your eyes and let your shoulders and head drop slightly forward. See how relaxed you feel? This simple exercise will help you to lower and control your anxiety level. You can do this one on the job. When you are anxious, take advantage of your breaks to get the privacy you need and do some deep-breathing exercises. It will give you relief. Remember, it comes through divinely designed means.

2. You can think yourself out of fear.

Second, apply some rational controls to your fear and anxiety. Subject your fears to the law of averages. Ask yourself, "What are the chances that what I fear will actually happen? What are the statistical odds I'm up against?"

This may not help the habitual worrier. He is like the man who stood on the street corner snapping his fingers for hours. Finally, someone went up to him and said, "We've been watching you standing there on the corner and snapping your fingers for a long time. We're curious. What are you trying to do?" "Oh," the man replied, "I'm keeping the elephants away." Hoping to relieve the poor man, his observer replied, "Sir, don't you know there isn't an elephant within two thousand miles of this place?" "Yeah," the finger snapper said gleefully, "you see, it works!"

Some people are convinced worrying works. Others have been brave enough to discover that the chance their worries will materialize is so small that it doesn't pay to worry. Paul shares this bit of practical wisdom with his readers in Philippians 4:6, "Be careful (anxious, full of care) for nothing."

I suppose relying upon statistical perspective can be carried too far. I once heard the story of a man so fearful of getting on an airplane with a bomb on it that he wouldn't fly. When faced with the fact that the only way he could include an important convention in his schedule was to fly, he was terrified. So, he called his friend who was an insurance actuary.

"Hey, Harry, this is George," he said. "You remember how I hate to fly? Well, I have to go to a convention next week and the only way I can get there on time is to fly. I'm terrified of getting on a plane with a bomb on it." "Oh, George," Harry said reassuringly, "people don't put bombs on airplanes." "Nevertheless, Harry, what are my odds?" George persisted.

Harry left the telephone to consult his tables. When he returned he announced confidently, "Relax, George. There's only one chance in a million you will get on a plane with a bomb on it." "I knew it," George replied. "It'll happen to me just as sure as I get on that plane. Isn't there anything I can do to improve my odds?" "Well, wait a minute," Harry said. After he had consulted his tables again he announced jubilantly, "Yeah, George, there is something you can do to improve your odds. Take your own bomb on board with you. The chance of you getting on a plane with *two* bombs on it is only one in *ten* million."

Try as we will, none of us can take all of the risk out of living. Living *is* risk-taking. But learning not to exaggerate your risks can lower your anxiety level.

The use of statistical perspective is also an effective way of managing our fear that other people won't like us. As with other unhealthy fears, this one also has to be faced to be conquered. If this is a source of anxiety for you, you might begin to manage it by asking yourself, "What are the chances that everyone I meet will like me?" An honest response to that question requires each of us to admit, "Zero." Then proceed to ask yourself, "Why should everyone like me?" Isn't that expecting too much of people? After all, not everyone who met Jesus liked Him. In fact, even of the twelve He chose to be His closest friends there were still two He couldn't count on—one denied Him and the other betrayed Him. You see, even Jesus could only depend on about 85 percent of His friends.

It would be nice if everyone loved you, but is it really necessary? If seven or eight out of every ten people you meet like you, isn't that great? With odds like that in your favor when you meet new people, assume they will like you. And be surprised when they don't. After all, I'm convinced if people knew me better they would love me more!

3. The Lord is your shepherd.

Learn to create Bible scenes in your mind when you are anxious or afraid. The Word of God is filled with restful, relaxing scenes. Often, calm can be restored to an anxious person through effective use of mental imagery. That's how I was able to help Gail.

An attractive woman in her late forties, Gail was highly intelligent and a devoted Christian. Yet, she could not drive herself to her sessions when she first began seeing me. She was frightened the moment she left her house, and became terrified by the bustling traffic on our expressways. She had to depend on her husband or a friend to drive her to her appointments.

In getting acquainted with Gail, I discovered she was very imaginative. Most people who are anxious and fearful have active imaginations, but they are focused on the wrong kind of mental images. Wanting her to discover how her imagination could work for her rather than against her, I asked, "Gail, what are your three favorite Bible scenes?" She listed them: "The Twenty-third Psalm, the Good Shepherd and the one lost sheep, and Jesus calming the storm on Lake Galilee."

"Good," I said. "Now, I want these scenes to minister to you. First, I want you to take three deep breaths." I gave her the same instructions I gave you earlier in this chapter. When she had finished her deep-breathing exercises, dropped her shoulders, and closed her eyes, I suggested,

"While your eyes are closed and you are enjoying such a good relaxed feeling, why don't you picture in your mind the one Bible scene you like most. When you have it in focus, tell me which one it is."

Gail's first choice was the Twenty-third Psalm. She worked with that scene until she could picture the green pastures, locate the stream, see the surrounding hills, hear the sound of the shepherd's staff and the bleating of the sheep. I also helped her develop her ability to fix her other favorite Bible scenes in her imagination.

Gail was instructed to take a few moments before leaving the house to recreate one of those scenes in her mind. Then I reminded her that each of them emphasized the reality of Christ's presence with her everywhere she went. By beginning to focus on an awareness of God's presence and assuring herself that she could do all things through Christ (Philippians 4:13), she was able to drive to her sessions after the first five weeks. By that time, she was also able to shop more comfortably.

Every person has some imaginative ability. You can create in your mind scenes you have seen on television or in the movies. Memories of faces and voices from your past remain accessible to you. Pleasant memories of family times and vacations are accessible to you. Using this ability can provide you a very practical tool for reducing anxiety.

4. Listen to God's reassurance.

Practice mentally focusing on reassuring passages of Scripture. Here are some examples:

> *Peace I leave with you, my peace I give unto you: not as the world giveth, give I unto you. Let not your heart be troubled, neither let it be afraid (John 14:27).*
>
> *Fear thou not; for I am with thee. Be not dismayed; for I am thy God: I will strengthen thee; yea, I will help thee; yea, I will uphold thee with the right hand of my righteousness (Isaiah 41:10).*
>
> *Ye are of God, little children, and have overcome*

them: because greater is he that is in you, than he that is in the world (1 John 4:4).

I can do all things through Christ which strengtheneth me (Philippians 4:13).

And we know that all things work together for good to them that love God, to them who are the called according to his purpose (Romans 8:28).

What shall we then say to these things? If God be for us, who can be against us? (Romans 8:31).

It is never God's will for us to be terrorized by circumstances. How do I know that? The Word of God tells me. In Matthew 28:20 Jesus says: "lo, I am with you alway, even unto the end of the world."

When the angel of the Lord announced Christ's birth to the shepherds, he first said, "Fear not." Why did he say that? He had come to give them detailed information about where they could find baby Jesus. Can you imagine how you would feel if you had been among those shepherds that night? Their routine work was interrupted by an angel. It's easy to understand why they were frightened.

Had the angel of the Lord not helped them to manage their fear, they never would have remembered where to find the Christ child. Fear fogs your memory—tends to make you forget.

At critical moments in our lives we are overwhelmed with fear and anxiety and tend to miss creative options for life decisions God wants to help us discover.

Now, let's see how approaching a common source of anxiety from a biblical point of view may help us manage it better. Many of the people I see miss their opportunities for a more abundant life in Christ because of self-consciousness. Do you know what self-consciousness is? It is the feeling of being observed, but not approved.

This feeling can be so uncomfortable and preoccupying that it can mentally paralyze you. Regardless of how experienced a speaker may be, if the people he is addressing begin to act disinterested, it becomes increasingly difficult for him to think clearly and to express himself well. Self-consciousness can be that crippling.

God has not made you self-conscious

Paul was concerned that Timothy might be overwhelmed by self-consciousness. That's one of the reasons he wrote a second letter to him. In the first chapter Paul says that Phygellus and Hermogenes, some of Timothy's contemporaries in Asia, had turned away from him. Paul wants to be sure that this doesn't happen to Timothy (2 Timothy 1:13-15).

He reminds Timothy that his faith is the product of three generations in his family. He challenges Timothy to greater enthusiasm in his ministry and assures him of God's help in giving a clear and unmistakable testimony of the gospel. Here's how Paul said it, "When I call to remembrance the unfeigned faith that is in thee, which dwelt first in thy grandmother Lois, and thy mother Eunice; and I am persuaded that in thee also. Wherefore I put thee in remembrance, that thou stir up the gift of God, which is in thee by the putting on of my hands. For God hath not given us the spirit of fear; but of power, and of love, and of a sound mind" (2 Timothy 1:5-7).

The Greek word translated "fear" can be more accurately understood to mean "self-consciousness." Paul's reference to a "sound mind" is not a concern for Timothy's mental health. He is assuring Timothy that God has equipped us with power and love which enable us to overcome the anxiety of self-consciousness so that we can think clearly, express ourselves clearly, and be effective in bearing testimony to Christ before the world.

If you are self-conscious, take 2 Timothy 1:7 as God's word to you. God has not made you self-conscious. The roots of your self-consciousness are deep in your past. In fact, you probably have no memory of a time in your life when you were not self-conscious.

Home environments which produce self-conscious children are created by parents who are difficult to please and who believe that children are to be seen and not heard. When a child brings home a report card of four A's and a B, they ignore the A's and ask, "Why the B?" Children raised in this kind of home feel they are always being observed, but very seldom approved.

"Come unto Me—I like you"

Paul assures Timothy that our heavenly Father is not like many earthly parents. He is observing us all the time, and most of the time He is approving of us in Jesus. This is a new kind of Christianity for many people. It has never dawned on them that God is pleased with their lives most of the time. In fact, many Christians are happy to get through a day when they feel like their heavenly Father is not displeased with them. For the most part, their goal is to avoid God's wrath.

Yet, the Bible makes it clear that God brags on His children. In Job 2:3 God says to Satan, "Hast thou considered my servant Job, that there is none like him in the earth, a perfect and an upright man, one that feareth God, and escheweth evil?"

Nothing will revolutionize your relationship with God more than understanding how easy it is to gain your heavenly Father's approval. After all, Jesus did not say, "Come unto me, all ye that labor and are heavy laden, and I will give you a nervous breakdown." He said, "Come unto me, all ye that labor and are heavy laden, and I will give you rest. Take my yoke upon you, and learn of me; for I am meek and lowly in heart: and ye shall find rest unto your souls. For my yoke is easy, and my burden is light" (Matthew 11:28–30).

God wants us to know that He is not only observing us all the time, but most of the time He is approving of us, in Jesus. What does that do to your self-consciousness?

Three kinds of power

Paul told Timothy that God has given us power, not fear and self-consciousness. What is this power God has given us? First of all, God has given us the power to be called His children. John 1:12 says, "But as many as received him, to them gave he power to become the sons of God, even to them that believe on his name." The Greek word John uses for power is *exousia,* which literally means "authority." God has given me the authority to become His child. No one becomes a child of God by human choice alone. Each one who enters God's family takes his place there by an expression of God's will.

The second kind of power given the Christian is defined by the Greek word *zoe*, for which the English translation is "everlasting life" or "eternal life." "For God so loved the world, that he gave his only begotten Son, that whosoever believeth in him should not perish, but have *everlasting life*" (John 3:16 italics added). This is the same power by which Christ, as the Word, made all things out of nothing. "All things were made by him; and without him was not anything made that was made. In him was life . . ." (John 1:3,4). What creative power! In Chapter 7, I will have more to say about its application in the affairs of our daily lives.

The third kind of power God gives us is the kind Christ refers to in Acts 1:8, "But ye shall receive power, after that the Holy Ghost is come upon you: and ye shall be witnesses unto me both in Jerusalem, and in all Judea, and in Samaria, and unto the uttermost part of the earth." Here the Greek word is *dunamis*, from which we derive our English words "dynamo" and "dynamite." Both of these words are energy-related. A dynamo provides a continual flow of energy, while dynamite is expressed in a sudden burst of energy. In giving this power to believers, Jesus provides the energy required for their expression of an effective witness to His gospel. Sometimes this may be expressed very boldly, but usually it takes the form of a light continuing to shine in the darkness.

The purpose of these gifts of power is to provide us with the courage to love. "For God hath not given us the spirit of fear; but of power, and of love . . ." (2 Timothy 1:7). As we experience this confidence and love, we discover the courage to overcome our self-consciousness and are able to reach out and confidently share God's love with those around us.

God watches you with loving eyes

When Isaac Watts was just a boy he lived next door to an elderly Christian lady who took a special interest in him. He sensed her love for him, so he visited her often. One day, she noticed how fascinated Isaac was with a Scripture motto on her wall. The passage came from Genesis 16:13. It was Hagar's prayer as she was cast out of Abraham's home. This short motto simply said, "Thou God seest me."

Because of his interest in it, the old lady decided to give Isaac the motto. As she took it down from the wall and handed it to him she said, "Son, I want you to have this. When you get older, you'll meet people who will want to make you believe that this Scripture means God is following you with a judgmental eye, watching everywhere you go. Seeing everything you do. Searching for some reason to judge you. Don't you believe them. For what this passage really means is that God loves you so much He just can't take His eyes off of you."

Your natural parents may have left you feeling like they were always observing you, but seldom approving you. You may have brought into your adult life crippling self-consciousness from your past. However, as a Christian you need to know that your heavenly Father does not view you that way. He is always observing you, because He loves you so much. And—most of the time—He is approving you!

In determining to defeat unhealthy fear in your life, you may want to make a list of sources of fear and anxiety: review the four methods for conquering fear we have discussed and determine which you believe will be most effective for you. In our example, we saw how biblical passages can be used in helping to reduce self-consciousness. The other methods suggested were:

1. **The use of deep-breathing exercises.**

2. **An application of statistical perspective to reduce exaggerated fear and anxiety.**

3. **The creation of restful biblical scenes in your mind for use in meditation.**

As you begin to apply these suggestions for dealing with the fears in your life, the Lord may help you to defeat some of them instantly. However, it is more likely that you will overcome most of them gradually. That's the way it happened for David. Early in his life, David said, "What time I am afraid, I will trust in thee" (Psalm 56:3). When he was older and had learned to overcome his fears, he wrote, "The Lord is on my side; I will not fear: what can man do unto me?" (Psalm 118:6).

Learning to come to terms with fears and anxieties will help you become more confident in your approach to life. This may result in your becoming aware of angry feelings you have been too anxious to acknowledge. Anger makes a good servant, but a poor master. In our next chapter I will suggest some practical ways for getting in touch with your angry feelings and putting them to work for you.

ANGER: MASTER OR SERVANT?

Many church people have a tendency to see any expression of anger as being undesirable. In fact, anger is often seen as a result of the fall of mankind.

However, before Adam and Eve fell, God gave them the commission to ". . . replenish the earth, and subdue it; and have dominion over the fish of the sea, and over the fowl of the air, and over every living thing that moveth upon the earth" (Genesis 1:28).

Without an aggressive drive, Adam and Eve would have been unable to subdue the earth or maintain dominion over it. Anger and aggression were part of the emotional equipment man was given for the task. Experienced and expressed in healthy ways, these provide the intensity and energy for an effective life.

However, as a result of the fall, anger has become one of man's worst enemies. Uncontrolled or misdirected, it can complicate or even destroy one's life.

Anger makes a poor master. However, it can be harnessed and turned into a productive servant. What follows has been written to help you break out of bondage to your anger and learn how to make it work for you.

You can't start too soon! As parental love relieves us of infant fears, each of us becomes secure enough to demonstrate anger. Any mother knows what infant rage is—once her soft, tender little bundle of love stiffens, reddens, and screams, she knows her little one has begun his lifelong bout with anger.

The limits parents begin to set on their infant's behavior inevitably frustrate him. If he has been loved enough to feel secure, he will vent his frustration in an angry test of those limits. Learning to manage such angry moments in ways that meet with his parents' approval is an essential survival lesson. In many homes when little people get angry it results in big people getting angry. And when big people in the home get angry, little people can't afford the luxury of being angry any longer. Sometimes it's a matter of timing. . . .

Perhaps you've already heard the following story. You'll agree that it illustrates beautifully the point I'm making. A mother heard her four-year-old son screaming and crying from the basement where he was watching his father build cupboards. Fearing the boy had been seriously hurt, she opened the basement door and saw him sobbing there on the steps. "What in the world is wrong with you?" she demanded. Through his tears her little fellow volunteered, "Daddy hit his thumb with the hammer."

"If daddy hit *his* thumb with the hammer, then why are *you* crying?" she asked. "Well . . . I didn't cry at first," her son admitted. "I laughed."

A child raised in this kind of home soon learns to hide his anger as much as possible. Children discover what their parents will not permit them to do when they are angry. However, most children get very little positive help in learning how to manage their angry feelings. Few parents are thoughtful enough to explain ways in which their child's anger can be expressed with the parents' permission. As a result, children often learn to feel guilty for *experiencing* anger and downright sinful for *expressing* it.

The national scope of this problem is seen in the 1974 Report of the Joint Commission on the Mental Health of Children:

> *The role of violence and its encouragement in young children must be faced squarely. Some children meet*

abuse and angry outbursts at the hand of their parents. Nearly all children are exposed to graphic violence over the television screen. Through possible imitation of and identification with these models, patterns of violent behavior may be easily acquired.

Of at least equal importance are the patterns by which the young child is taught to handle his own frustrations, his own angry feelings, and the constructive or destructive acts for which he comes to feel responsible. Possibly no other area represents as profound a source of pathology in our culture as the handling of anger and aggression.

Although children raised in Christian families should be subject to less family violence, they probably receive no more positive training in dealing with anger than their peers in secular families. If this statement startles you, then remember that being angry—to some Christians—means being "bad." With many, anger is not only a misdemeanor—it's a felony. When parents view anger like this, their response to it is likely to be punitive and suppressive rather than instructive.

However, the Bible does not treat anger that way. In Psalm 7:11, David reveals that ". . . God is angry with the wicked every day."

Believe it or not, the third chapter of the Gospel of Mark records that even Jesus *experienced* anger—and He *expressed* it!

The Pharisees wanted to find some reason to condemn Jesus. Finding Him in the synagogue on the Sabbath, they tried to trick Him. A man was there with a withered hand. The Pharisees watched to see if Jesus would violate the Sabbath by healing this man. It was obvious to the Lord that the Pharisees were more interested in keeping the Sabbath than in helping this poor, crippled man. This angered Jesus, and He decided to heal the man on the spot. Mark puts it this way:

And he entered again into the synagogue; and there was a man there which had a withered hand. And they watched him, whether he would heal him on the sabbath day; that they might accuse him. And he saith unto the

79

man which had the withered hand, Stand forth. And he saith unto them, Is it lawful to do good on the sabbath days, or to do evil? to save life, or to kill? But they held their peace. And when he had looked round about on them with anger, being grieved for the hardness of their hearts, he saith unto the man, Stretch forth thine hand. And he stretched it out: and his hand was restored whole as the other. And the Pharisees went forth, and straightway took counsel with the Herodians against him, how they might destroy him.   Mark 3:1–6

Anger is a normal human emotion

If God is angry with the wicked every day, and even Jesus experienced anger, then maybe our fear of our own anger and subsequent guilt are exaggerated reactions to a normal human emotion.

I want to share with you now a simple four-step formula for dealing with anger. By making this formula work for you, you can live more comfortably with your own anger.

1. Accept anger as a fact of your life.

Like the common cold, anger is a recurrent life experience. You may not like it, but you can't ignore it and stay healthy. It is the second emotion we learn to experience; only fear precedes it. As mentioned earlier, anger is first expressed as infant rage.

At that point, no guilt is associated with it. You have to learn to feel guilty for being angry. However, most of us were taught to feel guilty about our anger so early in our infancy that we cannot remember a time when we didn't.

Of course, when expressions of anger are undisciplined and destructive, it is healthy to feel guilty. Most of us are concerned about the dangerous side effects undisciplined anger may have. This is the issue Paul addressed in writing to the Ephesian church: "Be ye angry, and sin not: let not the sun go down upon your wrath" (Ephesians 4:26).

Unfortunately, instead of seeing this as a command from

80

Paul to learn healthy ways of managing anger, many believers have seen it as implying that good Christians never get angry. They take a very legalistic view of this passage, implying from it that if you get mad you're a "bad" Christian. And if you stay mad overnight, you're "really bad."

Actually, Paul is saying that as long as we are human we will have to come to terms with anger. He is urging us to learn how to manage it promptly, efficiently, and constructively. Then when we have learned healthy ways of handling our anger, we can put each day's conflicts to rest with the sunset.

"Yes you are!" "No I'm not!" "Yes you are!"

Christians who see anger as inconsistent with their faith must deny their anger or confess it as sin. Unfortunately, it is much easier to deny it. They can admit to being terribly upset, nervous, frustrated, irritated, disappointed or even furious much more easily than they can to being angry.

Can you imagine how ridiculous it must be to observe two such believers engage in a heated argument? As the conflict increases, voices are raised, the muscles stand out in one brother's neck, and a sharp edge comes into his voice. His face reddens—and then his more "spiritual" brother says condemningly, "Why, brother, you're *angry.*" And the other brother responds in a strained voice, *"I am not angry."*

Of course, any neutral observer of such a confrontation would realize that both men were extremely angry at the moment. However, admitting it would leave them feeling that they weren't very good Christians because of their mutual deeply-rooted conviction that "good Christians don't get angry."

Can you imagine the apostles arguing and debating the differences between the Jews and Gentiles in the church at the Council of Jerusalem without raising their voices? Recording that historic event, Luke honestly acknowledges

81

that the agreement reached only came about after there had been ". . . much disputing" (Acts 15:7).

The participants in this heated argument were not only "good Christians," they were apostles and elders of the church (Acts 15:6). There is no hint that this heated exchange of sharp differences was a negative reflection on their spirituality.

It is healthier to view anger as a normal human emotion that everyone must learn to accept and deal with in daily life than to pretend that it doesn't exist in the life of a healthy believer. The fact that you experience anger in no way implies that you should consider yourself less spiritual than others.

Perhaps it will be easier for you to develop this attitude if you begin to see anger for what it really is. In its simplest form . . .

Anger is unexpressed energy

Physiologically, this is exactly what it is. When your mind interprets some situation as threatening, a biochemical reaction is triggered which results in the creation of unusually large amounts of energy for your use in facing the perceived threat. Your emotion of anger is thus transformed into physical energy.

Think for a moment of what that means. Do you remember your high school physics class? Einstein discovered that under certain conditions *matter* can be destroyed—but insisted that *energy* cannot be destroyed; it can only be transformed.

Once you are angry you are in possession of energy which cannot be destroyed. Until you determine what form the expression of your energy will take, you have committed no sin. Your moral challenge is this: you are responsible to determine what you will do with the energy your anger has created.

If a person can't admit he is angry, he will have great difficulty learning healthy ways of discharging the energy his anger has created. Therefore, the first step in our formula for anger management is simply to accept anger as a fact of your life. Realize that you are entitled to experience anger without guilt or shame so long as you learn to express it appropriately.

When you are able to accept your anger, you may find it showing up at unexpected times. Often when people are grieving, they are aware of anger. They may feel so embarrassed and guilty about this that they can't discuss it even with their closest friend. Yet this is such a common experience that few people suffer the loss of loved ones without going through it. Their anger may not make sense, but it is real. Sometimes they are angry at their loved one for dying and leaving them. At times they are angry with God for permitting it to happen.

How do you help someone in these circumstances? Let them know these feelings are common among people going through similar circumstances. Encourage them to express their anger to God. You'll discover this is very difficult for them to do.

People fear that if they express anger to God He may in turn get angry at them. They have vivid mental pictures of how angry their parents became with them when they became angry as children. They must be reminded that their heavenly Father is not like an earthly parent who may respond to the child's anger by becoming furious with the child.

Sometimes it helps to communicate this truth to people with a little humor. One of our therapists puts it this way: "If you're angry with God, tell Him you're angry with Him! Go ahead and tell Him! He's big enough to take that!" Helping a person express anger to God and discover that it does not separate him from God's love is an important part of getting that person through his grief.

Now for the second step in anger management.

2. Become aware of your anger.

Unrecognized anger is far more dangerous to us than that which we are able to accept and recognize. When you learn to accept your anger, no one has to tell you that you're angry. You are aware of it. You know you're angry.

When you know that you are angry, you can choose from among several healthy and appropriate ways of expressing it. However, if you insist on denying your anger, you are likely to express it in ways that damage your relationships with the important people in your life.

Men are especially vulnerable to this deception. When it comes to recognizing our emotions, we men are at a real disadvantage. Our culture brutalizes us emotionally. We are taught to grow calluses on our feelings. When little sister falls down and skins her knee she comes crying to Mother or Dad for comfort. She is taken up in their arms, given some affection, and assured that everything will be all right. When brother falls down, he comes running to a parent expecting the same treatment. After all, his knee hurts just as much. But as often as not, the parent may take him by the shoulder, jerk him a little, and say, "Oh, hush! Don't you know big boys don't cry?"

In such informal ways as this, boys learn that a man in our culture is not expected to show his emotions. We expect our men to be "tough." Unfortunately, part of being tough or strong means that males must learn to be insensitive to feelings. This is part of the male's traditional preparation for bearing the brunt of the competition in our highly materialistic society.

Little girls are allowed to feel comfortable with being emotional but they still grow into women who most likely deny being angry. Little boys are taught to hide their feelings, which often results in them hiding *from* their feelings.

This difference in the way males and females are socialized is widely recognized among Americans. In fact, it is built into our sense of humor. Men jokingly remark that the woman's motto is, "If at first you don't succeed, cry, cry again!"

Take a personal safari

If you are going to become aware of anger in your life, you are going to have to go on a search for it and be determined to find it.

Begin to look for the places in your life where you think you may be unconsciously hiding anger. Look underneath words you may be using to disguise your anger. Catch yourself saying things like: "I'm fed up." "I've had it." "I'm sick and tired of that." "That burns me up." "I can't swallow that." "He makes me sick." "She makes me sick to my stomach." "I'm disgusted." "You make me laugh."

Here's one that really disguises the anger: "I'm *hurt*." We won't permit people who come to EMERGE to say they are hurt unless they are willing to acknowledge at the same time that they are angry. After all, how can someone hurt you without making you angry? People resist acknowledging this. They will say, "I'm just so hurt." And I will insist, "And angry." "Oh, no!" they object. "I'm not angry—I'm just hurt."

Then I explain, "If someone came in here and hit me in the face I can predict two simultaneous feelings would surface in me. One would be pain. The other would be anger. Yes, I would be hurt—but I would also be angry. Don't just recognize one of those feelings—acknowledge them both!"

Usually the person will say, "Well, when you put it that way, I can see what you're talking about. I guess I am angry as well as hurt."

Don't hide your anger from yourself

Unfortunately, the church has allowed believers to identify with the pain of a hurtful experience but not with the anger: it's okay for believers to say, "I'm hurt," but it's *not* okay for them to say, "I'm *angry*."

As a result of this kind of religious training, it is extremely difficult for Christians to say they are angry when their children are living contrary to the way they have been raised. Instead, they say, "My children are *breaking my heart.*" Who are we kidding? Of course, once in a while our children behave in ways that hurt us. But I can tell you without any hesitation that when my children hurt me they also tick me off. When they behave in ways that make me look like a failure as a parent, I'm not only hurt—I'm angry.

When I go to church I'm smart enough not to tell folks there that I'm angry with my child. I make sure I tell the people at church that I'm "burdened" for my children. Or, if I want to appear even more spiritual, I will say, "My child is *breaking my heart.*"

Of course, there's nothing wrong with simply sharing the pain of your parental experiences with your friends at church. However, you should know yourself well enough to know that mixed in with the pain and sadness of what you are experiencing is some anger. Even though you may feel it is socially desirable to hide this from others, don't hide it from yourself. You can deal with your anger much more effectively once you get it out in the open. Become aware of your anger.

Look for anger in episodes of depression

Depression is another hiding place for anger. More frequently than not, situational depression is aggravated if not initially caused by anger which the person unconsciously turns inward as a form of temporary self-hatred. However, depressed people seldom recognize themselves as being angry. They say things like, "I feel blue." "I'm really down." "I wish I were dead." "Sometimes I just feel like killing myself."

It never ceases to amaze me that people can be suicidal and still deny that they are angry. In an effort to put these desperate people in touch with their anger, I have said to them, "It must be very painful to be so angry with your-self," and had them reply in genuine amazement, "What makes you think I am angry with myself?"

Often they are unable to become aware of their anger unless someone directly points it out to them. Sometimes I have been successful in helping such a person see his hidden anger by saying something like, "Well, I've always believed that before you could bring yourself to kill someone you had to be very angry with him—even if that someone happens to be you." It is interesting to see some of these people as they get in touch with their anger toward themselves for the first time.

In most of the depressed people I have seen, there is a large amount of disguised anger. Once the person recognizes it and begins to become aware of it, they have taken an important step toward recovery. We'll pursue a more complete discussion of anger's role in depression in a later chapter.

Living with a depressed person can also be anger-provoking—but for different reasons. Years ago, when my wife was battling postpartum depression following the birth of our first child, I didn't understand what she was going through. All I knew was that I would come home day after day and find her depressed. At that time, I hadn't learned how to come to terms with someone else's feelings. I didn't know how to give her the emotional support she needed from me. This was frustrating.

When I would come home and find her still depressed I would say really brilliant things like, "Oh, no, not again!" Or, worst yet, "Honey, you know, I just don't know what to do. I try and try to be the best husband I can be and it doesn't seem to help."

Both of these statements are loaded with anger. I wonder how I was so blind as to not see it then. In the first instance, I was unconsciously trying to get my wife to hide her depression from me. It produced a feeling of powerlessness in me that was too painful for me to tolerate. In the second instance, I was hoping my wife would feel so guilty for presenting her "terrific" husband with such a depressed mate that she would just "snap out of it."

"They shall be comforted"

Then one day when I again found her on the verge of tears, the Holy Spirit prompted me to put my arms around her, tuck her head on my shoulder, and say to her, "Honey, go ahead and let your feelings out. You'll feel better when you've cried and gotten your feelings out of you."

Immediately she began to sob her heart out. I hadn't said anything magical, but when she was finished crying she had gotten some of her feelings out of her. She not only felt better, but I had grown considerably taller in her estimation because I had learned to communicate with her at the level of her feelings.

Since that time, I have become increasingly aware of how deceptive a person's mind can be in attempting to avoid angry feelings. If you want to become aware of your anger you must learn to look for it in places where you think it may be hiding.

Look for your anger in your nonverbal behavior. Are you an angry driver? How fierce are you in competitive sports? How do you react when you or your side loses in party games? How much do you grind your teeth? How do you react when someone keeps you waiting?

Get curious about where your anger may be hiding from you. You are much more likely to learn to manage anger maturely if you discover it early in its rise so you can go to work to control your anger before it overwhelms you.

"Oh, my aching back!"

Since anger affects you physiologically, learn to identify its buildup in your body. Get curious about what happens to you physically as you begin to get angry. Where in your body do you first become conscious of anger? I can feel my neck muscles tighten. My shoulders get tense. A sharp edge can be heard in my voice. People literally give me a pain in the neck.

Where do *you* experience anger? Some people first become aware of it in the cardiovascular area. Others develop lower back pain. Some experience anger in the gastrointestinal tract. Others have difficulty breathing. What happens in your body when you become angry? Where do you feel it?

Why is this so important? The earlier you detect the presence of anger, the sooner you can impose your spiritual controls for anger.

This brings us to the third step in our formula for anger management:

3. Control your anger.

Our maturity is measured by our ability to accept our emotions, become aware of them, and control them. The most mature man is the one who is most in touch with his feelings and who has best control of them. By accepting and detecting anger, a person can gain the advance notice he needs to impose his controls so as not to be embarrassed by an undisciplined display of anger.

In His Sermon on the Mount, Jesus makes it clear that the less control a person has over his anger the more serious are the consequences he must face:

> *But I say unto you, That whosoever is angry with his brother without a cause shall be in danger of the judgment: and whosoever shall say to his brother, Raca, shall be in danger of the council: but whosoever shall say, Thou fool, shall be in danger of hell fire.* Matthew 5:22.

Notice that if you are angry without a cause you are only in danger of "judgment." So far, you have said nothing. Once impulse control is lost and the friend is called an idiot, you are in danger of "the council." If you throw constraint

89

to the wind and curse your brother, then you are in danger of "hell fire."

The principle Jesus is teaching here is clear. The less control a person has over his anger, the more serious are the consequences he must face. This not only defines the way God deals with us, but it also usually defines the way anger management works in daily life. If you are in control of it, you don't usually suffer the serious consequences you suffer when it controls you. When your anger gets control of you, it can complicate your relationships and destroy your family. Therefore, conscious awareness of anger becomes important equipment in alerting a person to his needs for control.

Avoid clamming up

In your efforts to control anger, let me suggest that you first of all avoid "clamming up." People who attempt to control anger by clamming up risk damaging themselves. Psychosomatic illnesses feed on unexpressed anger.

God has not designed your body to accommodate large amounts of unexpressed anger over long periods of time. The energy created by the anger, conflict, tension, and pressure of the day needs to be released—as much as possible—before the day's end. If you don't develop ways of getting that energy out of you in nondestructive activities, sooner or later it will find symptomatic expression among the weakest of your organic systems. So, don't "clam up" and run the risk of damaging your physical health.

Avoid blowing up

The second extreme method of managing anger you will want to avoid is "blowing up." When you blow up, you damage your relationships. If you don't say it, there'll be nothing to forget. If you don't do it, there will be nothing to remember.

There are other, better ways of managing your anger than to resort to either of these extremes. First, learn to identify the *source* of your anger and determine if the *degree* of your anger is appropriate to the situation. Then . . .

Apply your controls

Build up a repertoire of control behaviors which seem to work reasonably well for you. Let me make some suggestions. Suppose you and your mate are really at it. You have reached that familiar point in your argument where you are both generating more heat than light. There doesn't seem to be any solution and you can feel yourself losing control. At that point, why not turn to your mate and say, "Honey, I need some time out. Give me a few minutes to cool off." Put some physical space between the two of you. Go to another room. Change your activity. Get busy doing something which can take your mind off things temporarily.

In all fairness, if your mate has the good sense to give you "time out" when you ask for it, then extend them the same courtesy. When you can see they are overloaded with tension, anxiety, and anger, give them some relief. Let them back out of the argument for a few minutes.

Another good control mechanism is to go for a walk. Notice, I am not suggesting you go for a drive. It is not safe to drive when you are extremely angry. However, going for a walk is an excellent way to cool off.

If you decide to use this way of regaining control, I hope your mate is not like the woman whose husband was about to attempt it. She yelled at him, "If you walk out of this house now, I'll follow you out on the sidewalk and scream at you until everybody in this neighborhood knows what I have to put up with!"

Assure your mate that your request for "time out" doesn't mean you are trying to avoid the subject of the controversy. If the matter is important enough to produce that much friction between partners it is too important to postpone indefinitely. However, once both partners have established a track record of good faith by picking up the discussion in better control at a future time, it should be easier to tolerate these delays.

Count on some storms

It is too much to expect that most couples can live together without these times of conflict. After all, how can a husband and wife know intense pleasure and intimacy without also knowing intense pain and conflict at times? Unfortunately, most Christians have the impression that if their marriages are what they should be, mates will seldom disagree and never have heated arguments.

Once in a while I see a couple who try to impress me by telling me, "Well, we may have our faults, but one thing our children will have to admit—they have never heard us raise our voices at each other." It may not be appropriate for me to challenge this statement at the time, but you can be sure I am saying to myself, "If they don't raise their voices at each other, how do they manage their anger?" Some quieter ways can be as damaging to a marriage as loud arguments.

If you are an intense person, you are not only intense in expressing your pleasure, but you are also intense in conveying your anger. And in those moments of intense pain and conflict between mates it is important to recognize the need for some time and space to regain composure. When we get away for a few minutes our emotions calm down and we can put a more rational perspective on what's happening. Then we can come back together, pick up the same subject, and resolve the difference without an explosion.

Each person needs some control techniques to rely on in moments of intense feelings. How many times do people say things to us which impulsively prompt some sarcastic reply? If we yield to the urge of the moment, a deeper and more painful difference is unnecessarily created. The next time you face such a moment, realize you need just a brief pause to help you control your impulses. Often something as simple as silently counting from one to ten will give you enough time and emotional distance to overcome your tendency to let them have your "zinger."

If counting from one to ten doesn't seem to be an adequate way for you to maintain control, then try saying the Lord's Prayer to yourself. Any simple behavior will work if it helps you avoid a hasty response you will regret later. I have met many people who would do anything possible to get back what they said in a moment of impulsive anger. Take time to develop some of these simple disciplines of control. With their help, you will experience the good feeling of getting through intense conflict with your self-respect intact and your anger in control.

God intends for anger to be your servant—not your master! Once you have accepted this emotion as a fact of life, have become aware of where your body registers it, and acquired some effective methods of control, you are in a position to direct the energy your anger produces into creative or recreational activities.

This is the fourth step in our formula for living with anger.

4. Direct your anger.

It is simpler to teach young children skill in directing anger than it is to teach adults. If you have children in the home, teach them some things they can do when they are angry and need to get rid of the energy their anger produces. Give them some toys they can pound. Put up a punching bag they can work out on. Build a pyramid of carpeted steps children can run up and down. Give them permission to be angry and a choice of energy-demanding activities they can engage in when they *are* angry so that their anger will not necessarily cost them your disapproval.

When your children choose to do things you have defined for them to do when they're angry, brag on them. Say things to them like, "I know you were very angry this morning, but it was really neat for me to see the way you managed your anger. I was really proud of that. How did you feel about the way you behaved?" Then listen to the feedback. It will help you know what they are thinking about as they learn to manage their angry moments. A simple plan like this can help your children grow up having control over their anger most of the time.

There's hope for adults, too! Even though your parents may not have taught you positive ways of dealing with anger, your heavenly Father can help you get control of your anger regardless of how old you are. Anyone who is willing to work at it can tame anger. God will help with the process.

Your needs for control will be put to the test in marriage. In marriage you not only have your own angry feelings to contend with at times, but you also have to learn how to deal with your partner in moments of his or her anger. Learn how to avoid unnecessarily triggering your mate's anger. Whether or not the bull charges is frequently determined by whether or not the red flag is waved. If the animal is snorting and pawing in the dirt, that's not the time to start waving your flag. If you do, you shouldn't wonder why the bull charges.

When you see your mate out of control, the wisest and most loving thing you can do is retreat. Give your mate a chance to regain composure. When things have settled down, if you have been that considerate, your mate will probably apologize. More important—your mate will have seen an example of the benefit that comes from gaining spiritual control over anger.

Parenthood has its own battlegrounds

Parents get angry. Parenthood pushes most of us beyond our limits of control at times. Perhaps the best way to manage such situations is to apologize to the child. Children are among the world's most forgiving people. The humiliation of having to ask your child to forgive you for letting your anger get the best of you should help you have better control in future dealings with the child. Your honesty in apologizing to your child also establishes a good base for requiring your child to apologize to other family members when he has lost his temper. The pain of having to ask others to forgive you is a tool your conscience can use to provide better control of anger in the future.

There's a place for healthy anger in parenthood. Just stay in control. Remember Jesus' mood when He chased the moneychangers out of the temple. Remaining calm and unruffled when your children have misbehaved in embarrassing ways would be failing them as a parent. However, try to remember the difference between "motes" and "beams." Don't pull out the cannon to go hunting for gnats. This kind of approach to young people frequently wins the battle, but loses the war.

Because teenagers can argue so eloquently in their own defense, some parents get drawn into shouting matches with them. Often only a minor point divides them, but once tempers are ignited, a major battle is waged. Such a situation reminds me of a preacher who reviewed his Sunday sermon outline and discovered that one point was very weak. Rather than strengthen or eliminate that one point, he chose to note in the margin, "Point weak. Shout here." When a parent has to get into a shouting match with a teenager it is an indication to the youngster that the parent's case is weak. If your case is strong enough, you don't need to shout to make it stick.

Learn how to keep your "cool" as a parent

Remember the three "Fs" of good discipline. Be *fair*. If the limits you have set for your teenager are fair, you don't have to shout to defend them. If the responsibilities you outline for your children are fair, you don't have to apologize for them. If they aren't fair, then no amount of loud talk will make them fair. Change them. Make them fair. Once you know you are being fair as a parent, you can afford to be *firm.* Many parents cannot be firm unless they are angry. However, you do not have to be angry in order to be firm. The fact that you know you are being fair should help you to be firm.

Be *friendly.* Teenagers are more likely to respect firmness that is friendly than firmness that is angry. Remember, they are masters of passive aggression: they know how to keep their cool while they are needling you into losing yours.

If you want to feel what it is like to have someone's passive aggression aimed at you, put yourself in one father's place. The family had been seated at the table several minutes waiting for the oldest son to take his place. At last, he rushed into the dining room. He sat down at the table and bowed his head. His father noticed that the boy's hands were filthy. He said to his son, "You know better than to come to the table with hands like that. Get upstairs and wash your hands." The family waited patiently for him. Finally, after several more minutes, his father impatiently shouted, "What are you doing up there that's taking you so long?" The son whiningly replied, "I'm only doing what you told me to do."

For a parent not to feel provoked by that kind of behavior is asking too much. However, I would hope that a wise parent would learn not to fall into that kind of trap, lose his cool, and lash out at the boy. It will take practice to refuse the bait. But the first time you succeed you will feel wonderful. Get wise to the tactics of your teenagers. Be sure your case is strong and fair. Once you know you are fair, then be firm—and be friendly.

It is God's will that energy created by anger be expressed constructively. If putting your anger into constructive action is a problem for you, let me give you some simple rules that will help you get on top of your anger.

1. Be determined to succeed.

First of all, be determined to succeed in controlling your anger. Say to yourself right now, "With God's help, I am going to have the control over my anger that I know He wants me to have. I am going to make it my servant, and not allow it to be my master."

2. Be willing to seem foolish.

Second, at the beginning of your effort, be willing to do some things which may seem foolish to you. Getting control of your anger may call for the temporary use of other innocent behaviors you may find foolish.

Several years ago a man came to see me because he was physically abusive to his wife. He would slap her, push her, shove her down, and if she tried to get away from him he would follow her and continue his abuse. Afterward he would be extremely apologetic and desperate to save his marriage. His wife finally refused to stay with him unless he got professional help.

As I often do in cases like this, I suggested he erect a tackling dummy in his basement. I taught him the four-step formula for anger management. Much of the anger he expressed in such instances was really displaced anger from earlier relationships. It was helpful in relieving his immediate symptoms to teach him to vent his unexpressed anger in some other physical activity consistent with his state of health. A tackling dummy served this purpose very well.

The first time I saw him after he had worked out on his tackling dummy he said to me, "You know, I feel kind of foolish punching that thing around."

I replied, "As foolish as you feel after you have beaten your wife?"

"No," he admitted with a smile. "Not that foolish. If I have to feel foolish I guess it's better to feel that way for hitting a tackling dummy than for hitting my wife."

"You guess so?" I asked.

"No," he conceded. "I know it's better than hitting her."

At times the biggest battle is getting the person to accept some substitute behavior until he can learn the spiritual, emotional, and intellectual skills necessary to control angry impulses.

I have found similar situations with women who abuse their children. When I suggest kneeling down by the bed and pounding their mattress as a substitute for abusing their children they look at me as though I am suggesting something to them that isn't Christian. It takes considerable effort to help such a woman understand that she can't destroy her anger. Once it has been created it is going somewhere. Once she sees that this is simply a temporary way of getting her anger expressed without harming anyone, she is able to accept it better.

You must "help yourself" to new behaviors

Typically, people in such situations expect you to be able to lay your hands on them, pray for them, and bring them some kind of miraculous cure without involving them in any effort to discipline their anger. Even though their habits have been ingrained over many years, they expect to have this behavior changed immediately and completely with little or no effort on their part.

It is difficult for many believers to associate prayer with anything less than total healing. Improvement with effort on their part appears to them to be more of a source of human help than divine.

Thank God for miracles! And where would we be without them? However, the fact that we call them "miracles" identifies them as exceptional and rare. If this was the typical way believers were to manage their emotional problems, such events would be happening far too frequently to call them miracles.

Paul spells out the process through which healing most often comes to us in circumstances like this:

Wherefore, my beloved, as ye have always obeyed, not as in my presence only, but now much more in my absence, work out your own salvation with fear and trem-

bling. For it is God which worketh in you both to will and to do of his good pleasure. Philippians 2:12,13

In the beginning of your battle with temper, realize this is a joint effort between you and God. Be willing to do some foolish things as a temporary step toward more mature ways of managing your feelings. Remember, the energy created by your anger can be used in many different ways. Believe God to help you wean yourself from tackling dummies and mattresses once you begin to learn the immediate relief that usually follows an innocent release of anger's energy. Then God will help you discover that the energy your anger created can be used in many constructive ways. It will scrub floors for you. It will build cupboards, wax woodwork, mow grass, and, if you have the heart for it, shovel snow.

If you prefer more recreational activity, your anger can be expressed in jogging, racquetball, golf, and any other sport you may find enjoyable. The more skilled you become in accepting and detecting your anger, the more capable you will be of putting its energy to healthy use.

Remember—anger is a poor master but a good servant.

Anger can furnish the motivation and energy for many worthwhile projects. Jesus directed the energy of His anger into His battle with the legalistic religion of the Pharisees. He held up to ridicule a religion that was more interested in seeing its rules kept than in helping people who hurt.

The reformers certainly made a friend of their anger and used its energy in their causes. Martin Luther said, "I can preach better when I'm angry." I don't recommend that for healthy pulpit preaching, but there are ways to harness the energy anger creates to build excitement, motivate people, intensify their interest, and spark their enthusiasm for worthy causes.

In getting control over anger in your life, be patient. This is not a single step of growth for most people. It is a journey. However, every journey must begin with a first step. Begin now to apply the simple insights I have shared with you in the management of your anger.

Remember, Jesus and the apostles directed the energy created during their angry moments into a project which gained for them the reputation of "these that have turned the world upside down" (Acts 17:6).

Multiply the productivity of your life. Convert the energy of your angry moments into activities which will bless God and benefit others. Do more than make a friend of your anger—make it your servant and God's servant.

Doing this will resolve a major guilt issue for many believers. In the next chapter, you will learn how to tell the difference between the healthy guilt the Holy Spirit raises in your conscience in order to keep you close to God and the unhealthy guilt the enemy uses to falsely accuse you.

5

COMING TO TERMS WITH GUILT

One day when I came back to the office after lunch there was a message for me to return a call from a man on the east coast. As he began to talk I could hear the anxiety in his voice. Fred was a young man still in his twenties. After the first few minutes of our conversation I knew the nature of his problem, even though I had not talked with him before.

He had an obsessive preoccupation with obscenities directed toward God. He believed this constituted an unpardonable sin. We see these symptoms frequently at our center. An obsession is an idea which persistently and compulsively intrudes into a person's thought life.

This particular obsession appears to be spiritual in nature because it involves obscenities toward God. However, the purpose of symptoms in emotional disturbances is to direct the person's attention away from their real problem.

Unfortunately, the symptoms usually create more pain and dissipate more energy than would be required to confront the source of their difficulty.

Fred's basic problem was emotional, not spiritual. He was suffering from unhealthy guilt which resulted from a need to condemn himself. Certainly, as an evangelical Christian, Fred's thoughts about God would give him all the evidence he needed to conclude that he had committed the "unpardonable sin," was the world's greatest sinner, and a rotten excuse for a human being.

What kind of unresolved problems in a person's past would result in such an exaggerated need to condemn himself? In most cases with similar symptoms, the person is struggling with unresolved sexual guilt. In view of this, you might think that the problem is basically a spiritual one, but it isn't.

Usually, in talking with these people you will discover one of two responses when you ask them if they have sought God's forgiveness for the behavior underlying their sexual guilt. Some will say they have asked God to forgive them many times, but they don't believe He has. Others will say they believe God forgave them when they first asked Him, but they cannot forgive themselves.

In the first instance, the person responds to his need to condemn himself by rejecting God's forgiveness. In the second, he refuses to forgive himself. In either event, he is fighting a losing battle with unhealthy guilt. Basically, the problem is more emotional than spiritual. That is, his issue is more within himself than between himself and God.

As you will discover later in the chapter, one of the distinguishing differences between healthy guilt and unhealthy guilt is that unhealthy guilt never yields to forgiveness, regardless of how often one prays for it.

The discerning believer knows that when this is the case, it is in direct contradiction to 1 John 1:9, "If we confess our sins, he is faithful and just to forgive us our sins, and to cleanse us from all unrighteousness."

God never visits unhealthy guilt on anyone. When a person is afflicted with guilt which confession does not relieve, often that guilt is self-imposed. The result is self-condemnation. This emotional need to condemn oneself becomes the primary target for the treatment I prescribe.

Since people who suffer from this type of problem are usually believers, I have found a biblical approach to their healing to be more acceptable to them, and therefore more likely to be effective.

I arranged a series of appointments with Fred. As I had first suspected, I discovered him to be suffering from unresolved sex-

ual guilt. In his case it was masturbatory guilt. Over ninety percent of young men, and over fifty percent of young women
practice masturbation prior to marriage.

Many young people do not feel guilty about this practice.
However, for many of those who do, it poses a major mental
health problem. Because the church is so divided over this matter, young people receive very little practical spiritual help for
managing masturbatory guilt, even though it is desperately
needed.

Actually, masturbation is not discussed in the Bible. Matters
which are critical to our salvation *are* clearly and completely dealt
with in Scripture; therefore, I have chosen to view masturbation
as a matter of private conscience. Romans 14 tells us that there
are many issues which should be dealt with this way.

In certain circumstances, other factors become involved with
masturbation and make it a biblical issue. For example, the use of
pornographic stimulation in the practice of masturbation is in
clear violation of Matthew 5:28 where Jesus says that "whosoever looketh on a woman to lust after her hath committed adul-
tery with her already in his heart." Or, if a married person
prefers masturbation to intercourse with his or her partner, then
he or she is guilty of defrauding the other partner. This practice
is in violation of 1 Corinthians 7:5 where Paul admonishes us as
Christian couples not to deprive one another.

With the above exceptions, if a person does not feel guilty
about the practice of masturbation, others should not attempt to
bring him into judgment. Paul talks about that in Romans
14:10,13.

Most of those who do feel guilty about masturbation, such as
Fred, have been taught that God will not forgive them unless
they quit. So they promise to quit if God will forgive them. He
forgives them, but they don't (or can't) quit. Now they assume
that God withdraws His forgiveness because they haven't been
able to quit.

Is this the way God deals with us about any other sins? If so,
then we are all in trouble. Who among us can quit everything for
which he needs to be forgiven? Have you quit everything for
which you have ever been forgiven? Of course not. Neither have

I. If God does not deal with us this way about other sins, why should such a special case be made of masturbation?

Such an approach is unsound theologically because it assumes forgiveness is based on our ability to stop some practice for which we feel guilty. Such a salvation then would be by our works, not God's. This approach is also unsound psychologically, because it creates an obsessive need to remember what it is you are not supposed to do. This keeps the subject on your mind—which preoccupies you with it, and makes it much more likely that you will do it again.

As I explained this to Fred, you could see relief come to him. In fact, simply discovering that others had similar struggles helped him not to feel so odd about himself anymore.

"What should I do when I do it again?" he asked. "Well," I said, "what do you do when you say things again that you promised God you wouldn't say anymore?" "I ask God to forgive me," Fred replied. "And you believe that He does," I reflected. "Sure," he confidently responded.

"How long have you been managing your verbal sins this way?" I asked. "Ever since I've been a Christian," he answered. "Why haven't you quit saying things you shouldn't?" I challenged. "I want to," he insisted. "I try."

"So, even though you haven't quit, God still forgives you as often as you ask Him because He knows you want to quit and you try. Do you suppose God would treat your problem with masturbation the same way He treats your problem with conversation?" I asked. "I never thought of it that way before," Fred said reflectively. "I believe He would." "So do I," I reassured him.

This became the basis of our treatment approach. Fred began to see that God was not condemning him. He was condemning himself. As he learned to bring this part of his life under the atonement, unhealthy guilt diminished. His preoccupation with obscenities toward God gradually disappeared. Today, he is married and enjoying an active place of Christian service in his local church.

Healthy guilt builds good character

The ability to respond to healthy guilt feelings by coming to terms with them honestly and resolving them in biblical ways is essential to building the believer's character. In time, a person's character is revealed by his attitudes and behavior. Knowing someone over a period of years, you learn the attitudes and behaviors which characterize him. Then, you can predict fairly accurately how the person will respond to different situations. This is what allows us to say of our friends, "He just wasn't himself today"; or, "I don't know what it is, but something is bothering her." Character is that observable and predictable.

Of course, once in a while, any of us can and will act out of character. That is, a person of bad character is capable of doing some good things. A habitual thief and liar may help an elderly person home with his groceries, but that doesn't make him a person of good character.

On the other hand, once in a while, a person of good character may do some bad things. For example, someone whose character has been above reproach for years may sexually misbehave over a brief period of time, but that doesn't necessarily change his basic character. A good person can do some bad things. This is difficult for some Christians to accept, either about themselves or others.

One of the tragedies of the church is that when good people have momentary lapses of character, the many faithful years they have invested in God's kingdom are so easily forgotten. There is a tendency to judge them harshly for behavior which is basically out of character for them.

Perhaps this is why Paul admonished the believers in Galatia, "Brethren, if a man be overtaken in a fault, ye which are spiritual, restore such an one in the spirit of meekness; considering thyself, lest thou also be tempted" (Galatians 6:1).

The power of your conscience

What makes your character so predictable? Your conscience. Your character is a product of your conscience.

The Bible talks about the relationship between conscience and character. Paul predicts, "that in the latter times some shall depart from the faith, giving heed to seducing spirits, and doctrines of devils; speaking lies in hypocrisy; having their conscience seared with a hot iron" (1 Timothy 4:1,2).

In 1 Timothy 1:18,19 Paul reminds Timothy of the spiritual fate of those who abandon conscience. "This charge I commit unto thee, son Timothy, according to the prophecies which went before on thee, that thou by them mightest war a good warfare; holding faith, and a good conscience; which some having put away concerning faith have made shipwreck."

Where does your conscience come from?

God has given the capacity for conscience to every human being. Romans 2:14,15 make this clear: "(For when the Gentiles, which have not the law, do by nature the things contained in the law, these, having not the law, are a law unto themselves: which show the work of the law written in their hearts, their conscience also bearing witness, and their thoughts the meanwhile accusing or else excusing one another)."

Your conscience is a divine mark which sets you off from brute beasts. Every normal person is born with the capacity for conscience. However, the content of your conscience (those things you associate with right and wrong) is culturally derived. Therefore, the kinds of things for which each of us feels guilty will be greatly affected by the part of the world in which we were born and the particular area of the country in which we were raised.

For example, Americans eat beef, but those who live in Hindu countries would consider this to be a sacrilege. On the other hand, they might eat dog, which Americans would find most repulsive.

In the South, where I was raised, we were taught to address older people with respect. "Yes, ma'am." "No, ma'am." "Yes, sir." "No, sir." These were courtesies ingrained in my conscience as a child which I discovered didn't usually exist in the consciences of the northern children I met in Ohio where we moved when I was in my teens. So, you see, your conscience is not only affected by the country in which you were born; it is also affected by the particular part of that country in which you were raised.

Three qualities of a good conscience

One of the most valuable gifts you can receive from your parents is a good conscience. What is a good conscience? How do you define it? Here are three qualities by which a good conscience can be identified.

First of all, a good conscience is neither too broad nor too narrow. It won't let you get away with too much, but it won't condemn you for too little. A good conscience will not let you be comfortable in breaking the law, or offending the important relationships in your life.

Second, a good conscience is consistent in its vigilance. It grants its approval and imposes its sanctions regardless of time or place. It will not be conveniently silenced.

Third, a good conscience is forgiving. Once you respond to the pangs of a good conscience with confession, and, if necessary, some form of restitution, it won't hurt any longer. It will let you be at peace with God and yourself.

How does a good conscience grow?

For a moment, let's look at how your conscience is formed. Conscience develops out of our interaction with our parents during the first five years of life. It emerges as parental love selectively alleviates infant fears. Initially, this interaction between parent and child centers largely around the amount of physical space given to us as infants.

Your brain associates pain and pleasure with place. Any pediatrician will verify this observation. As a profession, pediatricians have done everything possible to make children less apprehensive in their offices. Most pediatricians no longer wear a white coat in the office. They have taken the medicinal odor away. They have surrendered their hypodermic syringes to their nurses. They

107

provide little gifts for their patients. But, as long as our infants get their immunization shots in that office, we can expect them to scream out their predictable protests while they are there.

Their brain associates pain with place. Regardless of what is done to neutralize that place, their brain tells them that sooner or later they are going to get it "in the end."

The physical experiences of pain and pleasure become associated with the emotions of fear and love. We fear the places where we experience pain and we are fond of the places where we experience pleasure. This simple mechanism becomes the cradle of conscience.

You can give your child a healthy conscience

By avoiding certain definable extremes and following a very simple three-step formula, parents can be assured they are giving their child a healthy conscience.

Look first at the extremes to be avoided. Be sure the limits you set for your child are not too broad. Allowing a child to walk all over the furniture and to talk disrespectfully to adults is not in the child's best interests. Giving too much physical and emotional freedom produces a child other people can't stand. It also sets such broad limits for conscience that the child, later in life, will be without the protection and prodding of painful warnings when values and ideals are about to be violated.

On the other hand, avoid setting limits for your child which are too narrow. This results in your child seeing you as being very difficult, if not impossible, to please. Often, having to deal with such narrow limits produces a guilt-prone child who is displeased with himself much of the time.

Inconsistent limits are the most devastating. A child subjected to this kind of environment is unsure how to feel about himself, because he is unsure how his parents feel about him.

Now that we've looked at the extremes to be avoided, let me give you the simple formula we referred to earlier. You are most likely to create a healthy conscience in your child when you set limits according to these standards:

108

1. Be fair.

Parents will often ask, "How do I know when my limits are fair?" I simply reply, "Put yourself in your child's place. Then ask yourself how much liberty you could safely manage."

This application of Christian compassion toward your children is one of the most practical ways I know to test the fairness of your limits.

2. Be firm.

Firm limits which are fair help to produce a sense of loving security in your child. It's part of our fallen nature to test—and protest, from time to time—any limits on our behavior. So, don't depend upon your child's pleasant acceptance of your limits to indicate their appropriateness. Remember how vigorously you protested limits your parents set for you when you were a child.

After all, if they are fair you should be able to enforce them without feeling you are being cruel to your child. Any healthy person must learn to live within limits. The sooner we learn that in life, the better.

3. Be friendly.

Unfortunately, some parents only know how to be firm when they are angry. Without knowing it, they are teaching their children to delay any compliance with their limits until the parent's voice reaches a certain level reflecting the unmistakable look of anger. "How many times have I told you? The answer is *no*. Don't you understand that? It's spelled n-o. No!" This kind of harangue is not necessary. Remember what Paul says in Colossians 3:21: "Fathers, provoke not your children to anger, lest they be discouraged."

Gently, but firmly, enforce your limits. "I'm sorry that you feel so angry because I said you couldn't go. But it's my job to set the limits for you. It's your job to come to terms with them. All of your protests aren't going to change what

109

I've decided, so why don't you get busy doing something that will take your mind off this?"

Such a response establishes the parent's control, but it also helps the youngster learn how to accept limits without being too preoccupied by their frustration.

As a parent, how healthy is your conscience? What are the things that make you feel guilty? A healthy conscience will impose guilt when you are engaging in behavior which endangers your life, your character, your property, or the life, character, or property of someone else.

Once conscience is formed, it is highly resistant to change. For most of us, that is a blessing. We have had loving parents who gave us a healthy conscience. Even after we have established our own personal faith in Christ we do not have to struggle with a faulty conscience.

Our conscience may have had to be retrained through Scripture so that it is sensitive to the limits placed upon the believer's behavior by the New Testament. However, once this has been done, it continues to be a consistent monitor of our behavior—rewarding us when we obey Christ's teaching and reprimanding us when we disobey. A healthy conscience plays a prominent role in determining the extent to which Christ is reflected in our attitudes and behavior.

How to treat a sick conscience

The resistance of the conscience to change presents some Christians with an urgent need for spiritual healing. Their conscience is unhealthy. If you find yourself in this group, here are some A–B–C's to help you facilitate the needed change.

1. Acknowledge your need for healing in this area of your life.

How do you know if you need healing for your conscience? By looking carefully at the role guilt has played in your past.

Some have come into the kingdom with lives characterized by a lack of discipline. They have been dominated by habits, attitudes, and behaviors which have demonstrated a callous disregard of others in pursuing their own pleasure. All of this has precipitated little, if any, guilt in them.

These people need to have their conscience narrowed and strengthened to help them have better control over their attitudes and behavior. Unfortunately, people with this problem seldom seek help for themselves. When we see them in clinical practice it is usually because their behavior has brought others such pain that some kind of treatment is demanded.

Among our treatment population we are more likely to find Christians who are suffering from a conscience which is too narrow. That is why I have chosen to give this problem special attention later in the chapter.

2. Believe that God can help you correct a faulty conscience.

After all, if God can make you His child, He can do anything. If He can perform the miracle of regeneration in us, then certainly He can heal a sick conscience. The Bible provides us with beautiful examples of believers who experienced healings of conscience.

First of all, let's look at Jacob. His conscience was too broad. He bought his brother's birthright and stole his brother's blessing without experiencing enough guilt to inhibit him. In Jacob's all-night wrestling match with the angel of the Lord, his conscience was healed. From that time on Jacob experienced too much emotional pain to continue his devious ways. The God who changed Jacob's character from that of a deceiver to one who had power with God (which is what *Israel* means) can touch your conscience and help you change your character.

Second, there was Mary Magdalene. Before she met Jesus, there is no indication that she suffered guilt for earning her living as a prostitute. However, when she came to Christ He healed her conscience and changed her life.

Third, Paul underwent a real transformation of conscience. When he became a Christian he was driven by a

Pharisaical conscience. He was a legalist of the legalists. Here's how he pictured himself: "If any other man thinketh that he hath whereof he might trust in the flesh, I more: circumcised the eighth day, of the stock of Israel, of the tribe of Benjamin, an Hebrew of the Hebrews; as touching the law, a Pharisee; concerning zeal, persecuting the church; touching the righteousness which is in the law, blameless" (Philippians 3:4–6).

Can you imagine what a harsh, judgmental conscience Saul of Tarsus must have had before Christ touched him? Yet, sometime after his conversion and before he wrote his first letter to the Corinthian church, a miracle of inner healing took place in Paul's life. He describes the transformation which this brought to his conscience this way: "For though I be free from all men, yet have I made myself servant unto all, that I might gain the more. And unto the Jews I became as a Jew, that I might gain the Jews; to them that are under the law, as under the law, that I might gain them that are under the law; to them that are without law, as without law, (being not without law to God, but under the law to Christ,) that I might gain them that are without law. To the weak became I as weak, that I might gain the weak: I am made all things to all men, that I might by all means save some" (1 Corinthians 9:19–22).

What tremendous flexibility is now evident in this old Pharisee's conscience. How did this psychological miracle happen? The Jesus who transformed his life healed his conscience and changed his character.

3. **Concentrate your spiritual efforts on any transformation of conscience you may need until the necessary correction is made.**

Your spiritual life will only be as healthy as your conscience. So, keep working at it!

Healthy vs. unhealthy guilt

The person who will have the greatest struggle in his battle for a healthy conscience is the one whose conscience is too narrow and rigid. Often, such people are afraid they won't feel guilty enough to be saved. Their conscience is a tyrant. They will need to learn the difference between healthy and unhealthy guilt if they are ever to overthrow its impossible yoke. Let's take a look at three characteristics which define that difference for you.

1. Unhealthy guilt is rooted in rules, healthy guilt in relationships.

I grew up around a religion of rules. Unfortunately, I can't remember as much attention being focused upon a violation of relationships as on breaking the rules.

It was against the rules to play on Sunday. Even during the week we couldn't play the Old Maid card game unless we pulled the drapes to be sure we wouldn't be a stumbling block to someone who might look through the windows and think we were playing "cards." I was afraid to play pinball machines because if Christ were to return or if I should die before I had a chance to repent, my salvation could be in jeopardy.

The Christians in Galatia were prone to this kind of legalism. Even though Paul brought them out from such bondage, persuasive teachers attempted to put them under the bondage of the law again. That's why Paul wrote to them: "Stand fast therefore in the liberty wherewith Christ hath made us free, and be not entangled again with the yoke of bondage. . . . For, brethren, ye have been called unto liberty; only use not liberty for an occasion to the flesh, but by love serve one another. For all the law is fulfilled in one word, even in this; Thou shalt love thy neighbor as thyself. But if ye bite and devour one another, take heed that ye be not consumed one of another" (Galatians 5:1,13–15).

A legalistic faith tends to make judges out of believers. In such a frame of mind it is easy to be more concerned about keeping rules than maintaining relationships. Unhealthy guilt will preoccupy you with concern for rules and allow you to neglect your relationships.

Healthy guilt inflicts pain to warn you that important relationships are being threatened by your attitudes and behavior. The Pharisees were concerned that Jesus keep their rules, but He was more concerned about the state of their relationship with God.

Take time to survey the important relationships in your life. How healthy are they? What is the state of your relationship with God? How much of yourself have you invested in the interest of healthy family relationships? Who are your closest friends? Are you caring for those relationships?

These are the vital issues of your life. A healthy conscience will force you to face them honestly. When you are neglecting these relationships a good conscience will inflict enough emotional pain on you to bring these matters to your attention. When you address them responsibly, a healthy conscience will not only reward you with relief, but will also give you the kind of commendation which leaves you feeling good about the priorities of your life.

2. Both healthy and unhealthy guilt carry with them a compulsion to confess.

The key to distinguishing the difference between healthy and unhealthy guilt is in the kinds of things you are being driven to confess. Honestly ask yourself whether the issues being raised by your conscience are vital to a healthy relationship with God and with the people who are important to you. Remember, Jesus teaches us that an unhealthy conscience cannot distinguish between "motes and beams" and "gnats and camels" (Matthew 7:3; 23:24).

3. Unhealthy guilt never yields to forgiveness, but healthy guilt always does.

I often ask people suffering from unhealthy guilt, "What is it that you've done to prompt this awful, unrelenting guilt?" The most common response is, "I don't know."

Many of these people tell of long sessions of prayer during which they beg God to show them what is wrong in their life. As soon as someone tells me this I know their guilt is not from God. You and I may hold things against each other without revealing what it is, but God is not like that.

Husbands and wives are likely to play these kinds of games with each other. What couple hasn't headed home from some social gathering with the wife seated so far from her husband that if it weren't for the door she would be outside the car? When he inquires, "What's wrong, honey? What did I do? What did I say? Why—why are you so upset?" she folds her arms in obvious disgust and poutingly responds, "If you don't know, I'm not going to tell you!"

Of course, husbands are just as capable of playing the game their way. In a similar situation the man may back out of the drive like a maniac, peel rubber as he heads for home, and fill the car with eloquent stony silence. His wife, attempting to relieve the situation, may say, "I know I must have done something wrong, dear. What did I do? Wh—what did I say? What's wrong?" The man's thundering response is likely to be, "You know what's wrong!"

A person suffering from unhealthy guilt thinks God is like that. He thinks he has to beg Him to tell him the source of his guilt. Nothing could be farther from the truth!

If the guilt you experience is from God, He will be specific in identifying the source as soon as you ask Him. God does not play games with us. The only reason the Holy Spirit ever inflicts the pain of guilt is to safeguard your relationship with God and the important people in your life.

The purpose of the pain of conviction is to bring you to the place of forgiveness. As soon as corrective actions are taken in your attitudes and behavior to remove any threat to important relationships in your life, the pain God inflicts upon you will be gone.

Remember, "If we confess our sins, he is faithful and just to forgive us our sins, and to cleanse us from all unrighteousness" (1 John 1:9).

Guilt that remains after you've honestly confessed your sins to Jesus Christ is the work of a sick conscience. The

115

result is a sick need to suffer for what Christ died to save you from. It is tragic to see people insist on punishing themselves for some mistake of their past. They seem to believe that their willingness to suffer somehow impresses God with the sincerity of their grief.

Evelyn's story illustrates this. When Evelyn first came to see me she was in her forties. She had been on tranquilizers for years. After each of her first few sessions she would say, "I know there's something I have to tell you, if I am going to get better, but I just don't have the courage. I'm afraid you'll lose all respect for me once you know."

I reassured her that it was highly unlikely she would tell me anything I hadn't heard many times before. However, her secret had accumulated so much anxiety through the years that she simply could not bear facing it.

Finally, she opened a session by announcing, "This is the day. I made up my mind to get this whole business out of me today." Here is her story.

When Evelyn was a teenager, she became sexually involved with a young man from her church. Unfortunately, she conceived. When it became obvious she was pregnant, the pastor forced her and the young man to come to the platform during the morning worship service and confess to a crowded sanctuary that they had sinned. (By that time it was apparent to everyone.)

In spite of this humiliation, Evelyn and her boyfriend stayed in the church. The young couple married and, with their families' help, they began to build a stable marriage. To spare their first child (Margie) all the embarrassment they could, they managed to have the date on her birth certificate changed. Other children were born.

Through the years, Evelyn and her husband became respected members of the community and leaders in their church. However, Evelyn's sick conscience continued to pain her over this unfortunate mistake of her youth.

Evelyn's best friend, in whom she had confided during the trying weeks of her first pregnancy, moved away shortly after Margie was born. A few months before Evelyn came to see me, this woman's husband was transferred back into the area. Evelyn's youngest daughter, Becky, and her friend's youngest daughter had developed a close relationship. Evelyn's big fear was that this woman would feel a moral obligation to tell Becky the story of Margie's conception. There were moments when Evelyn knew her friend would never do this; however, much of the time she was tormented with this fear.

Once Evelyn had told me this whole story, I said, "Is that all?" She cried, "Is that all? Isn't that enough?" I assured her, "Evelyn, I've heard that story many, many times. Did you ask the Lord to forgive you at the time?" "Oh," she sobbed, "I asked God to forgive me then, and I've asked Him a hundred times or more since then."

"Do you believe He has forgiven you?" I asked. "Oh, sure. I believe God has forgiven me, but how can I ever forgive myself?"

As I became aware of the tremendous toll this unhealthy guilt had extracted from Evelyn's life, I became angry at the enemy. Just as Jesus said, Satan had stolen years of emotional peace from this child of God (John 10:10). I felt anger in my voice as I said, "Oh. The blood of Jesus was adequate to satisfy the holy nature of God, but it's not good enough for *your* holy conscience. Is that what you are telling me? Must God send another Son to die for *your* holy conscience? Isn't one Calvary enough?"

By this time Evelyn was sobbing uncontrollably. I heard her say through her tears, "My God, I've never seen it like that before." That day it dawned on her. Unconsciously, she had been trying to suffer for her own sins; "But he was wounded for our transgressions, he was bruised for our iniquities; the chastisement of our peace was upon him, and with his stripes we are healed" (Isaiah 53:5).

God healed Evelyn that day. Her medical doctor began to withdraw her from tranquilizers upon her next visit to his office. I saw her for follow-up visits at three- and six-month intervals. The healing that came to her that day could have been hers years before. After all, the guilt she had needlessly inflicted upon herself was borne by Christ for all of us.

There's something insidious about a person like Evelyn being unable to forgive herself. Usually, such persons are the last ones in the world to think of themselves as idolaters. Yet, they are worshiping an idol. How many times do you suppose such people have said to themselves: "Oh, if only it hadn't happened that way. How different my life might have been. But now it can never be what it might have been. My whole life is ruined."

These people are worshiping the "me-that-might-have-been." Because the "me-that-might-have-been" can never be, they refuse to accept the "me-that-is." And since they won't accept the "me-that-is," they can't discover the "me-that-can-be" in Jesus.

Such an attitude toward life is like that of a little girl who has dropped her china doll and broken it. Her mother picks it up and carefully mends it, but the little girl refuses to take it back because she knows it has a crack in it. Instead of focusing on the fact that she has her doll back, she keeps her eyes glued on the crack. Her doll is her idol.

When you won't forgive yourself of some mistake in your past, you're making an idol out of the "me-that-might-have-been." If you will smash that idol, and forgive yourself, God will help you discover the "me-that-can-be" in Jesus. Only by letting go of the past will you reach the future that can be yours.

Some people find this such a battle that they spend much of their life depressed. This kind of situational depression is very different from biochemical depression. In the next chapter I will give you some ways to tell them apart and I will share some suggestions for dealing with depression.

6

DEALING WITH DEPRESSION

Whenever I help a person deal with depression, it's more than just a clinical task for me. I remember the struggle my wife had early in our marriage. Shortly after the birth of our first child, she suffered a serious postpartum depression.

I knew she loved God. She has always had a very consistent devotional life. And yet, there was something apart from her spiritual life that she just couldn't deal with.

She recalls this as a time in her life when she had no conscious awareness of God's presence. She believed that our newborn son and I would be better off without her. For six months she wanted to die and sought opportunities to take her life. For several months after that, life would be a world of dark skies for her.

It's impossible to describe the powerlessness and helplessness I experienced as I sought every way humanly possible to be of some help to her, only to discover that nothing seemed to work. However, I did learn the importance of allowing her to express her feelings to me. And, even though she couldn't believe it, I never permitted myself to doubt her recovery.

I'm happy to say that God eventually healed her. And out of the pain of that experience I was driven to the Scriptures to study what they had to say about the issues of mental health and depression in particular. I think you'll be surprised to discover the people in the Scriptures who suffered from depression—and the ways God helped them deal with it.

What is depression?

Depression, as a form of human suffering, has been around for a long time. In fact, it's probably as old as man himself. It is the most common form of emotional pain. Most of us will have to learn how to come to terms with depression at some time in our life.

People frequently ask, "What is depression?" "Who suffers from it?" "What are its symptoms?" "How can a person deal with it?"

To give you some idea about how long depression has been around, it was Hippocrates, in the fourth century B.C., who gave us our first clinical definition of it. He identified depression as the "black humor" which he called "melancholia."

Today the National Association for Mental Health defines depression as "an emotional state of dejection and sadness, ranging from mild discouragement and downheartedness to feelings of utter hopelessness and despair."

Such a clinical definition of depression lacks something for those who have experienced it. If you have known the pain of depression you have a far more realistic understanding of it than can ever be put into words.

Do Christians get depressed?

Among church people, there seems to be a widespread notion that "good Christians" don't get depressed. If a person experiences deep depression it is suspected that he is guilty of some dark and hidden sin. Somehow, Christians are expected by many of their peers to live above all forms of discouragement or depression.

I remember the unnecessary pain this point of view caused my wife and I while we were going through her difficult postpartum depression. (I say "we" because, when your mate is seriously depressed you are affected by it also.)

We were young evangelists. We couldn't find a pastor who understood our mental health problem. And, we couldn't find a mental health professional who respected our faith. Our Christian friends advised us, "Just get into the Word and pray." The counsel of the mental health professionals was, "It's your religion. That's what's making your wife mentally ill. If she gets rid of that she will be rid of her problem."

Many people suffer from such unnecessarily narrow points of view. A healthy faith can alleviate many of the anxieties and tensions of the mentally ill. On the other hand, many Christians can benefit from the competent care of mental health professionals who respect their faith. It is gratifying to see more and more pastors and mental health professionals discover this.

I knew my wife was not suffering because she neglected Scripture reading and prayer. She was spending twice as much time in these exercises as I, and I wasn't depressed. Also, I knew that her faith was too important a part of her life for her to be helped by abandoning it. She needed the support of a healthy faith *and* competent mental health care.

Bible characters suffered from depression

Even a casual reading of Scripture reveals that many devout believers have suffered the agony of deep depression. The oldest book of the Bible tells how depressed Job was. Tornados had blown down his buildings and killed his children. Thieves had stolen his herds. His health was gone. He had lost everything he had.

Job was so overwhelmed by his sense of loss that he withdrew into seven days of silence (Job 2:13). Can you imagine being so depressed as to sit for seven days without uttering a word? He cursed the day he was born and wished he were dead (Job 3:3,11). His wife, not knowing how else to comfort him, encouraged him to curse God and die.

Remember, this was the man God bragged about to Satan (Job 1:8). He was literally the best man in the world. If such a man as Job was not above being depressed, certainly you and I have no reason to feel guilty when, as Christians, *we* get depressed.

In their depression, believers have no difficulty understanding how Job could feel as he did. Those same kinds of thoughts have rushed through their heads.

Elijah was another great man of God who had to do battle with depression. He had called fire down from heaven one day and rain on another. Yet right in the middle of this spiritual high, depression struck. Elijah found himself sitting under a juniper tree bemoaning his life and wishing he were dead.

He became so paranoid that he began to believe he was the only prophet in all Israel who was true to God. He had to be reminded that seven thousand others were as devout as he (1 Kings 18,19).

After Jonah had preached such a powerful sermon that the whole city of Nineveh was converted, he became so depressed that he sat down under a temporary shelter he had made and prayed for God to take his life (Jonah 4:1-9).

So, you see, no depth of spirituality nor degree of perfection makes you immune from depression. The fact that you may need to seek professional help for relief from this pain does not reflect negatively on your relationship with God. If medication is needed, you should be able to take it with no more guilt than if you were fighting infection.

What are the symptoms of depression?

The symptoms of depression will vary with its intensity. Most of us experience the "blues" from time to time. The zest goes out of life. We feel sad and dejected. We may retreat into temporary silence and reflect a surly mood.

These normal "downs" of life last only a day or two. As a rule of thumb, our therapists tell people to accept any depression that doesn't last longer than four days as a normal bout with the "blues." Any depression that lasts much longer should be given professional attention.

As depression deepens, physiological processes become involved. A person may suffer loss of appetite. Sleep disturbance is common. Difficulty in going to sleep, interrupted sleep and early awakening are often reported. A person's normal sex drive wanes or temporarily disappears.

When depression is primarily a product of disturbed biochemistry, frequently one or both of the following symptoms appear:

1. The person exhibits pervasive anhedonia, that is, a total absence of pleasure.

Nothing makes them happy or brightens their mood. They could hear that one of their loved ones, for whom they had prayed for years, had come to Christ, and give no evidence of joy. They could learn that they had suddenly become wealthy, and exhibit no emotional response. Their sense of humor is gone. They are incapable of pleasure. Knowing this can save you the frustration of trying to cheer them up.

2. The person presents an unresponsive mood.

A normal person reacts emotionally to the mood of the group he is with. Even a situationally-depressed person can be cheered up temporarily by the people around him. However, many biochemically depressed people remain impassive and oblivious to the mood of their social environment.

However, the most serious symptom of depression is the presence of suicidal wishes. Contrary to popular opinion, people who commit suicide do talk about it. In fact, it is rare for someone to commit suicide who has not communicated his intentions in some way.

If any member of your family seriously thinks about or talks about committing suicide, the safest thing you can do is to get them to a professional person who can measure the suicidal risk.

If your loved one needs to be hospitalized for his protection, urge him to consent to it. If he won't, you take whatever legal steps may be required to give him the protection he needs. It is better to tolerate the protests of his reluctance to hospitalization than to live with the regret of any negligence on your part.

I have never known depression to kill anyone. In the vast majority of cases, if the depressed person can be given the protection he needs during the most despairing time of his illness, he will survive. A chronically-suicidal person eventually may succeed in taking his life, but as a family member or mental health professional, I want to be sure I have taken every step I can to prevent it.

What causes depression?

Depression is often a secondary symptom of physical illness. That is why a competent professional person will want you to have a physical examination before assuming that your depression is psychologically induced. If there is some physical problem, it is important that it be treated. Often, the successful treatment of your physical problem remedies your depression.

However, just being a member of our modern society makes you a candidate for depression. If you can take the pace of life today without ever getting depressed, thank God and know that you are unusual. Most of us have our "down times."

A serious loss can also trigger a depression. This kind of situational depression may follow the death of a loved one, a divorce, or bankruptcy. It can also be precipitated by the loss of a lover, a friend, or a job. The loss of the ability to bear children depresses some women. Often, both men and women experience depression upon retirement.

Depression can come from painful circumstances in life: marital tension, personal illness, parent-child conflict, work aggravations, boredom, frustration with friends, or parental insensitiveness. Each of us has his share of these.

When we are going through these times it is easy to add to our discomfort by adopting unnecessarily distorted and exaggerated views of the situation. Then we find ourselves in the predicament of the man whose world was caving in. Angered at the simplistic advice he was receiving, he complained to his friend, "People keep saying to me, 'Cheer up! Cheer up! Things could be worse.' So, I've cheered up. And see, things have gotten worse."

Unfortunately, some people adopt a negative view of themselves and their world long before they start to school. It's not their circumstances which depress them; it is their view of life. From childhood they have viewed other people in a more favorable light than themselves. Their value judgments are predictably negative. They are overly critical of themselves and others. They see what is wrong rather than what is right about whatever they happen to be looking at. If you showed them a donut they would see the hole.

Once I saw a cartoon of an old western town. There was a banner over the main street bearing the name of the place—"Donut Center." Underneath the name, some kids had scrawled, "What a hole!" It is this kind of person who lives there. You may have to spend a few days in such a place, but don't become a citizen.

As you journey through life,
Let this be your goal:
Keep your eye on the donut,
And not on the hole!

How to deal with depression

Here are some suggestions for dealing with depression:

1. Don't let the fact that you're depressed, get you down.

Fear of depression, or guilt for being depressed, will only add to your discomfort. Remember, depression tends to feed upon itself. That is, you can become more depressed by dwelling on the fact that you are depressed. Try not to make a big production out of your depression. Assure yourself that a few weeks, or at the most, a few months will see you through it.

2. If you haven't had a thorough physical examination in the past six months, get one.

Even if nothing significant is found, at least you know that your depression is not symptomatic of some physical illness.

3. Learn the therapy that comes from staying busy.

You may not be able to escape your depression entirely, but it is not something you want to feed. Once you start to feed depression you will discover it has a ravenous appetite; and, the more you feed it the bigger it grows. That is why the worst thing a depressed person can do is to brood. Whenever you can, resist the temptation to dawdle and daydream. Plunge yourself into activities.

4. Discover the relief that comes from sharing your burden with the Lord in prayer.

David learned this secret centuries ago. In Psalm 55:22 he wrote, "Cast thy burden upon the Lord, and he shall sustain thee. . . ." Take the time to read Psalms 58 and 59. Notice how openly David shared his feelings with the Lord. He didn't pull any punches. He said it just like he felt it.

For David, prayer became a therapeutic way of venting his anger and bitterness. He cries, "Break their teeth, O God, in their mouth: break out the great teeth of the young lions, O Lord. Let them melt away as waters which run continually: when he bendeth his bow to shoot his arrows, let them be as cut in pieces. As a snail which melteth, let every one of them pass away" (Psalm 58:6–8). Can you imagine the relief that came to David as he emptied these feelings out before the Lord?

In Psalm 59, feeling overwhelmed by his enemies, he expresses his anxiety over his future. There is no attempt to cover up his bitterness and contempt. He prays, "Deliver me from the workers of iniquity, and save me from bloody men. . . . They return at evening: they make a noise like a dog, and go round about the city. Behold, they belch out with their mouth. . . . For the sin of their mouth and the words of their lips let them even be taken in their pride: and for cursing and lying which they speak. Consume them in wrath, consume them, that they may not be: and let them know that God ruleth in Jacob unto the ends of the earth" (Psalm 59:2,6,7,12,13).

Learn to trust your bitter, angry, hostile feelings to God. There is nothing you can feel that you can't express to Him in prayer. Find a private time and place for pouring your heart out before God. Never fear that an honest disclosure of your deepest feelings to God may alienate you from Him. You may have found it necessary to hide certain things from your parents when you were growing up, but there is nothing you cannot share with your heavenly Father. His courage to be transparent with his feelings in prayer endeared David to God as a man after His own heart

(Acts 13:22). God longs for that kind of a relationship with each of us; one which finds you "casting all your care upon him; for he careth for you" (1 Peter 5:7).

5. Share your burden with a friend.

Talking helps. My heart goes out to people who grew up in homes where children were to be seen and not heard. As adults, they are likely to be very private people who keep their problems to themselves. They tried talking when they were younger, but no one wanted to listen. So, now they are convinced that talking doesn't help. But it does! Let me prove it to you.

Suppose you and three of your friends get in your car and head home after a night of fellowship. As you approach the highway, you make your entry safely and start down the road.

At the first major intersection some fellow darts out in front of you. You have to swerve off the road to miss him. You almost have a wreck.

Now, what are the chances that you and your friends will proceed on your journey without some comment? Remember, there is no intellectual need to discuss it. You are all intelligent adults. Each of you saw everything that happened. None of you can add to the others' information.

In such a situation, I'll venture that you wouldn't get a quarter-mile down the road until one of you would excitedly ask, "Did you see that idiot?" From strictly an intellectual point of view that is an absurd question. Of course, everyone in the car saw "that idiot."

However, before that question could be answered someone else would anxiously observe, "Wow! We almost got it."

It's highly likely that you would continue to talk about your close call as you traveled down the road together. Probably, one of the first things you would say to your family after arriving home would be something like, "We almost didn't get here. We could have all been killed."

Why carry on all this conversation if talking doesn't

help? Well, the truth of the matter is, talking does help. It helps to reduce our level of anxiety. It helps to lighten our burden. That's why Paul instructs us, "Bear ye one another's burdens, and so fulfill the law of Christ" (Galatians 6:2).

When words are used as God intends, they decrease our pain and increase our pleasure. Healthy conversation within yourself and between you and a trusted friend can go a long way toward shortening the night of your depression and hastening the dawn of the new day you so long to see.

Surviving deep depression

My wife endured a very deep depression. Often, there is a significant biochemical involvement in such cases. If you've ever gone through a deep depression with a family member, you know you reach a point where you can no longer communicate with him. You try, but it's as though he can't hear what you say.

It will be easier for you to relate to your friends or loved ones compassionately if you understand that they would communicate with you if they could, but they can't. It is not so much that they are unwilling to communicate as it is that they are unable to. Assuming that they could communicate if they would, but they won't, simply generates more frustration and anger on your part, making it more difficult to be compassionate toward them.

Be patient. In time, you will observe an obvious mood lift in them. Then, efforts to communicate will be much more likely to succeed.

Medical assistance

Today, there are medications which can help alleviate depression and shorten its duration. These are especially effective in helping with biochemical depression. This type of depressive illness is sometimes referred to as endogenous depression, and often can be controlled through medication in much the same way as other chronic biochemical disorders such as diabetes, thyroid deficiencies, etc. The medications frequently used are the tricyclic antidepressants and some form of lithium carbonate. Had these medications been available when my wife was suffering her depression they could have brought her noticeable relief and considerably shortened that miserable period of her life.

Our center takes a conservative view toward medication. However, under competent medical supervision, we have found it helpful in most cases where people are suffering from moderate to severe depression. People who are taking medication for depression should be encouraged to take it as long as the doctor believes it is necessary, and at approximately the same time each day so that at all times it can be as evenly distributed in the body chemistry as possible.

Often, depressed people neglect their medication. Some may even resist it as a symbol of their illness. That is, the fewer pills they take the more healthy they see themselves to be. On the other hand, the more medication they take and the longer they take it, the sicker they see themselves to be. Of course, this is not an accurate perception of their situation.

In fact, if they reduce their medication, or cease to take it before they have recovered sufficiently to function fairly comfortably without it, their condition will very likely worsen. If medication is part of the treatment it is important that it be prescribed by a competent physician, taken according to his instructions, and terminated only under his supervision.

Nonmedical helps

The treatment God gave Elijah for his deep depression is still sound. You can read about the regimen in 1 Kings 19:5-8. "And as he lay and slept under a juniper tree, behold, an angel touched him, and said unto him, Arise and eat. And he looked, and, behold, there was a cake baked on the coals, and a cruse of water at his head. And he did eat and drink, and lay down again. And the angel of the Lord came again the second time, and touched him, and said, Arise and eat; because the journey is too great for thee. And he arose, and did eat and drink, and went in the strength of that meat forty days and forty nights unto Horeb, the mount of God."

First of all, notice that this treatment plan called for Elijah to be temporarily relieved of all his vocational responsibility. Today, such a goal is usually accomplished by hospitalizing the person. One of the primary benefits of hospitalizing the severely depressed person is to give him total rest.

Second, Elijah was put to sleep. Depressed people tend to extremes in their sleep patterns. Some have great difficulty with sleep. They may not be able to go to sleep. Once asleep, they may wake up frequently during the night, or they may waken an hour or two before their normal rising time and be unable to go back to sleep. On the other hand, some depressed people want to sleep most of the time.

Of course, neither of these extremes is healthy. However, adequate sleep is an essential part of any successful treatment program for depression.

Third, diet was a part of Elijah's treatment. A properly balanced diet is important in any recovery plan for depression.

Fourth, renewed spiritual vitality was at the heart of Elijah's treatment. Any Christian who has been depressed understands how important this element is to recovery.

I never will forget how my wife's battle with depression came to an end. We were holding evangelistic meetings in Beckley, West Virginia. The pastor and his wife had gone to make some hospital calls. Dolores and I took advantage of our privacy to kneel for family devotions. That morning, while we were praying, she experienced a consciousness of God's presence. This was the first time in six months she had been free from the horribly haunting feeling of being totally forsaken of God.

There was nothing special about that morning to indicate what would happen. I certainly didn't expect anything like that to happen. I believed that she would get better. In my heart, I knew that she would be aware of God's presence again some day, but I made no special effort to determine that it would happen that morning. But it did! That morning God touched her and lifted those heavy black clouds of depression from her.

This became obvious to me when she rose from her knees and came over to embrace me. There was energy in her face, a gleam in her eye, and a lift in her voice as she said, "Honey, the Lord touched me this morning, and I feel so much better." What a celebration we had!

It would be several months before depression would be an uncommon thing in her day, but its back was broken that morning.

For the Christian who is battling depression, it is important to celebrate any bright spiritual moment as evidence of God's help in the recovery process. However, care must be taken not to overreact to it. If a person attaches an exaggerated meaning to such moments and assumes they indicate an immediate end to the depression, any return of depression is likely to devastate his hope of recovery.

The pattern of recovery for most people involves a gradual emergence from depression. They have a few minutes free from it and begin to think, "Oh, I'm beginning to feel like my old self again. Finally, I'm getting this depression behind me." Then, right back into depression. And they say, "I thought I was over it. I don't know whether I will ever get over it." But, they have a little longer period of relief and again prematurely conclude, "Well, this is it. This time the depression is gone for sure." But it's not; and they're discouraged again.

However, little by little the periods of relief grow longer and more frequent. The periods of depression are less frequent and less intense. Most often, this is the pattern we see as a person recovers from deep depression.

Long-range goals for the depression prone

Some Christians must have total success in every venture they undertake or they feel totally defeated. However, there is something to be said for even moderate improvement in those situations where total success may not be achieved.

If you are a depression-prone person and would like to be as free from depression as possible, let me suggest some long-range goals for you. Please understand that reaching these goals may not eliminate depression in your future, but it can minimize the toll it takes from you.

1. See the advantages of depression.

For many people, depression is a primary way of coping with stress. As such, it is far less damaging than coping with it cardiovascularly or gastrointestinally. When these systems become the primary focus of stress, permanent damage can result to the vital organs involved.

So, as a means of coping with stress, depression has some advantages. Once the misery of the mood has lifted, you are not as likely to have damaged your body as are those who manage stress more somatically.

2. Learn to creatively manage your angry feelings.

Often, a large component of depression is anger trapped within a person and turned against him. When Sue came to see me, she had been depressed during the Christmas holidays for years. She couldn't understand this. Sue and her husband had a good marriage. Their children were healthy. The family was full of love. They enjoyed being together.

However, Sue's depression spoiled much of the joy of Christmas for the whole family. She wanted to do something about it, so we began to search for the source of her holiday depression.

Sue grew up in a large family. Her mother was an alcoholic. She remembered how, when she was a child, she dreamed of having a happy Christmas, but it never happened. Her mother was always drunk. There was no money for presents. Christmas was one of the most unhappy times of the year for her. She could remember thinking, "I hate my mother. If she wanted to, she could make Christmas nice for us—but she would rather get drunk."

She had never dealt with this anger. Sue needed an opportunity to acknowledge it and get it out of her; she needed help in forgiving herself for holding all that anger against her mother for so many years. Finally, she had to be helped to forgive her mother. When these issues were dealt with, Sue and her family had their first depression-free Christmas.

Once you are willing to acknowledge the fact that anger is playing a significant part in your depression, you have gone a long way toward doing something constructive about it. See if you can identify what it is you are angry about. Then, refer to Chapter 4 for some suggestions about how to manage your anger.

3. Work on adopting a positive world view.

Remember, the same glass of water which appears to be half empty to some, appears half full to others. Why not join the group that sees it half full?

You can test the nature of your world view by noticing what aspects of the world's future you focus on. What phases of Bible prophecy most intrigue you? When your view of the future is positive, you assume, "This world hasn't seen its best days yet, and neither have I!"

Paul prescribes an effective thought filter for those who want to focus on the positive in life. In Philippians 4:8 he writes, "Finally, brethren, whatsoever things are true, whatsoever things are honest, whatsoever things are just, whatsoever things are pure, whatsoever things are lovely, whatsoever things are of good report; if there be any virtue, and if there be any praise, think on these things."

4. See the divine potential in other people.

Learn the thrill of seeing God in the lives of your family members. See Him in the circumstances of your friends' lives. Of course, the fortunes of this world and the power of Satan are at work in our lives too, but you have a choice of where you want to fix your focus.

Having a positive view of life has nothing to do with closing your eyes to the evil realities around you. You see them. You know they exist, but you do not choose to focus on them. You choose to focus on Christ "because greater is he that is in you, than he that is in the world" (1 John 4:4). The author of Hebrews says it so well: "But now we see not yet all things put under him. But we see Jesus . . ." (Hebrews 2:8, 9).

Remember, Jesus is the door into life in another dimension. Don't be content merely to step out of an old life. Be determined to step into a new one. In the next chapter, I will share with you some of the exciting discoveries which await the Christian who is determined to explore his new dimension of life in Christ.

7

You Can
Live in a
New Dimension

Life can be better for you if you learn to make your spirit the dominating force in your life. Many people allow their lives to fall into the mold of their physical and emotional desires. Generally, they do what they feel like doing. Others often feel driven by life rather than being in control of it. Circumstances and other people determine their course. They do what they have to do to survive.

However, the Lord can help you turn that around. He can help you put your spirit in the driver's seat of your life, with Him at the controls.

Donna discovered this secret when she faced impossible odds. When I first met her she was single, in her teens, and living in a wheelchair. The doctors gave her little hope of surviving. She had suffered polio as a child, and now she was locked into an apparently losing battle with tuberculosis.

"The doctors say I'm gonna die," Donna volunteered as I arrived at her bedside. "It's not their fault. They're doing the best they can."

"What do you think about what the doctors have told you?" I

asked. "I think they're wrong," she said with a twinkle in her eye.

That was over thirty years ago. Donna is still going strong. Her doctors were wrong.

But that's not all. The doctors discouraged her from getting married, and told her she could never give birth to a child. They were wrong again.

In a day when some able-bodied people have difficulty finding one suitable mate, Donna has had two. Donna's first husband loved her very much. He took care of her as long as he lived, and gave her two lovely children, one son and one daughter. Both are grown now. Their father is dead, and Donna has since married another man who thinks the sun rises and sets on her.

The last time I saw Donna she was at a church where I was speaking. After the service we had a few moments to reminisce. "Donna," I said, "the first time I saw you I didn't think you were going to make it."

"I know," she snapped back with a chuckle. "You were just like the rest of them doctors. But I fooled you, didn't I?"

"You sure did," I admitted. "Now, if somebody told me you were dead, I wouldn't believe them."

"Well, it's just the Lord," Donna said humbly. "He's the one. He's brought me through."

That's the truth. God provided the healing in her life. But Donna played a role in her own survival, too.

The part she played is one that each of us can learn. You see, Donna learned how to keep her feelings from dominating her life. Now she has risen above the clumsiness and awkwardness of her crippled body. She refuses to be dominated by emotions which would give her little to feel good about. Much, if not most of the time, her spirit has been in the driver's seat of her life.

Prayer is the door

Prayer can open this new dimension of life to you. How sad it is that many believers never discover this. They approach prayer in a very traditional, ritualistic, and unimaginative way. For them, prayer remains a way of giving God His orders for the day. In fact, some have lists arranged just to be sure they don't miss anything. And when God doesn't do *what* they want Him to do, *when* they want Him to do it, they get angry with Him.

Such immature Christians seem to believe that God exists to do their will. Otherwise, why would they blame God for the bad things that happen to them—and the good things which don't?

Make no mistake about it—God encourages us to make our requests known to Him. But He also wants us to learn to trust Him more for our material needs instead of badgering Him daily with our lists.

Many of the things we pray for would come to us even if we didn't ask for them. Jesus teaches us that the material things God's people need will come to us as by-products of putting Him first in our lives. Once we learn to trust Him for our material needs, our prayers can be directed toward the more important issues of life.

In Matthew 6:31-33 Jesus tells us about a way of praying which can effectively change our lives and thus help us change our world. He says, "Therefore take no thought, saying, What shall we eat? or, What shall we drink? or, Wherewithal shall we be clothed? (For after all these things do the Gentiles seek:) for your heavenly Father knoweth that ye have need of all these things. But seek ye first the kingdom of God and his righteousness; and all these things shall be added unto you."

I call that creative praying. When your spiritual priorities are in order, less of your prayer time and energy is wasted in prayer spawned by unhealthy fear, anger, and guilt. You are better prepared to benefit from the opportunities of life. Your spirit leads—not your physical and emotional needs.

What *is* creative praying?

As you pray creatively, you assume the material world to be a product of the spiritual world. This is not to infer that if you only pray, everything you need to survive will magically come to you. It simply means that matter is not of an eternal nature. Spirit is. Spirit preceded matter in existence. In fact, all matter has come from spirit. Everything that exists, every material thing—every particle of matter, every gas, every form of life—has come into being because God, who is spirit, willed it to be.

In Hebrews 11:3 the author observes: "Through faith we understand that the worlds were framed by the word of God, so that things which are seen were not made of things which do appear."

Science has taught us to believe in the power of the invisible. The universe of the atom cannot be seen by the naked eye, but it contains the keys of life and death for this planet. The Scriptures teach that beyond such invisible dynamics of the physical sciences are unseen spiritual forces responsible for creating and sustaining the universe. John tells us that one of those is *zoe* (John 1:4). This is the Greek word for "eternal life."

Eternal life is now!

Many Christians think of eternal life as a kind of existence which will begin for them when they die or when Jesus returns. For example, the other day I heard a well-intentioned preacher refer to a believer's death as his "having entered into eternal life."

All of us look forward to the future expression of our eternal life, but I want to help you discover what this dynamic gift from God can do to enrich your life now. Once you understand the nature of eternal life, it will be easier for you to benefit from its present function in your life. It will be very much a part of the "sweet by-and-by"; however, it can be just as real in the "sweet here-and-now."

Eternal life is the creative force from which God made the entire universe. John describes that manifestation of God's power in creation like this: "In the beginning was the Word, and the Word was with God, and the Word was God. The same was in the beginning with God. All things were made by him; and without him was not any thing made that was made. In him was life; and the life was the light of men" (John 1:1–4).

The Greek word translated "life" in this passage is not *bios*, which refers to natural life. *Bios* appears eleven times in the New

Testament and each time it clearly refers to natural life. This word is *zoe*. It occurs one hundred thirty-four times in the New Testament. In over one hundred twenty of these passages it obviously refers to a kind of life that is supernatural. This is the power through which Christ made all things from nothing. It is spiritual and invisible in nature, but so powerful that the material universe is simply one of its manifestations.

John tells us further that this creative force has always resided in Jesus. It was His manifestation of that life-creating power in the beginning that resulted in all things being made out of nothing.

Jesus, as the eternal Word of God, is the source of this creative life, or energy (*zoe*), from which everything that is made has come.

With this understanding of who Jesus is and what eternal life is, read John 3:16,17: "For God so loved the world, that he gave his only begotten Son, that whosoever believeth in him should not perish, but have everlasting life. For God sent not his Son into the world to condemn the world; but that the world through him might be saved."

What does this famous gospel text say to you? Its meaning is obvious, isn't it? As God's love gift to this planet, Jesus came to give access to eternal life to all who believe in Him.

Why did God need to send that love gift?

In the beginning, God created man capable of mentally responding to this invisible creative force. This is manifested in Adam's power of creative choice. Before his fall, he was able to name all the animals (Genesis 2:19,20).

However, when Adam chose to eat of the tree of the knowledge of good and evil, as he assumed the awesome responsibility of moral choice, he also forfeited his access to eternal life. That part of Adam's spirit capable of responding to eternal life became dead in "trespasses and sins" (Ephesians 2:1).

This is the death God warned Adam of in Genesis 2:15–17. "And the Lord God took the man, and put him into the garden of Eden to dress it and to keep it. And the Lord God commanded the man, saying, Of every tree of the garden thou mayest freely eat; But of the tree of the knowledge of good and evil, thou shalt not eat of it; for in the day that thou eatest thereof thou shalt surely die."

This state of spiritual death has been transmitted from Adam to his offspring so that "in Adam all die" (1 Corinthians 15:22). However, God's love for mankind is so great that He offered His Son Jesus to die for the sins of Adam and his race. By accepting Christ's death and resurrection as an atonement for his sins, anyone who wants to can be born again (John 3:17).

What part of you becomes born again?

The part of you that is born again is that part of your spirit and mind which has been dead as a result of sin. Once you are born again, you are capable of responding to eternal life. Your regenerated sensitivity to eternal life enables you to experience the love of the Father, the triumphant presence of the Son, and the teaching ministry of the Holy Spirit.

Remember, eternal life is an invisible force which radiates from God. When you are born again, your spirit is sensitive to this force as it stimulates your mind. You begin to think in terms of life options that enhance and develop your divine potential.

Remember that your spirit is also sensitive to sin as it impacts on your mind. Sin stimulates your brain to think in terms of life options that detract from and destroy your divine potential.

Many Christians I see in counseling have trouble relating these spiritual forces to the daily issues of their lives. They do not understand that there is a spiritual dimension to their thoughts. Thinking is such a common experience to them, they assume it to be totally a natural process.

However, temptation and divine suggestion—both supernatural in origin—present themselves to each of us through our thoughts. Temptation is the product of an invisible force emanating from Satan which we call sin. Divine suggestion results from the invisible force emanating from God which we call eternal life.

Unfortunately, the average church member is more aware of

temptation than he is of divine suggestion. Since he is so unaware of divine suggestion in his life, he often feels overwhelmed by the complexities and ambiguities of today's world.

As a result, he often suffers from uncomfortable levels of anxiety. A practical understanding of the power of eternal life and how it enters into his daily decisions can eliminate much of this anxiety.

For centuries, Christians have believed that human history is shaped by two spiritual forces—satanic and divine. Although most agree that both of these powers are governed by the providential love of God, Christians have differed over how much personal freedom exists and where human responsibility lies within their jurisdiction. However, there is general agreement that man is sufficiently free to be held responsible and accountable before God for his behavior that results from his interaction with these spiritual forces.

The Bible illustrates how human decisions often were involved in the execution of providence. Reflecting on this aspect of history, Golda Meir, former prime minister of Israel, is said to have jokingly complained, "Just think, if Moses had turned left rather than right after he crossed the Red Sea we would have had all the oil and they [the Arabs] would have had all the rocks!"

As God providentially rules the course of all human history through His access to man's decision-making process, so He wants to guide each of us in the critical decisions of our daily lives. "For as many as are led by the Spirit of God, they are the sons of God" (Romans 8:14).

Through creative prayer the believer becomes aware of spiritual activity in his thought processes and develops the ability to know the difference between those thoughts resulting from sin, those originating from eternal life, and those suggested by his own natural thought processes.

Scripture stored in memory is an invaluable tool in this process. And whether you consider Hebrews 4:12 to refer primarily to the written Word of God or the living Word of God, its truth remains: "For the word of God is quick, and powerful, and sharper than any two-edged sword, piercing even to the dividing asunder of soul and spirit, and of the joints and marrow, and is a discerner of the thoughts and intents of the heart."

Skill in discerning the spiritual origin of your thoughts develops as the living Word is enthroned in your spirit and the written Word is stored in your memory.

Why should a person engage in creative praying?

The idea of eternal life as an invisible force capable of stimulating creative thoughts and choices for life may sound mystical to some. However, belief in invisible natural forces is a commonly accepted part of life. Wind, a vacuum, and electricity are just a few examples of invisible natural forces which have a profound impact on us. This is possible because we have discovered enough about their principles and properties to benefit from their power.

Creative praying is based on the assumption that invisible spiritual powers are at least as active in shaping the events of our world as are invisible natural forces, and just as predictable in the ways they operate.

The Bible defines the principles and properties of the invisible spiritual forces we call sin and eternal life, so that we can benefit from an understanding of their relationships to the practical issues of our everyday lives.

Through your study of Scriptures and in prayer, you can become more aware of these spiritual forces. You can learn more about how they impact on your thought processes and how they affect your choices which, in turn, shape your life and destiny.

1. Creative prayer makes you a new creation.

Creative praying changes us from children of Adam to children of God (John 1:12). We never pray a more creative prayer than when we pray to be born again. Acknowledging our personal need of atonement through Christ's death and resurrection not only makes it possible for us to be forgiven; it also enables us to become dead to sin and alive to eternal life.

We become more and more dead to the destructive options for living that sin stimulates in our minds; at the same time, we are becoming more and more conscious of the creative options for living suggested to our minds by "eternal life." This is what "putting off the old man" and "putting on the new man" is all about. Paul refers to this process as being "renewed in the spirit of your mind" (Ephesians 4:23). There is no greater miracle than this!

If you met Christ after reaching adulthood, can you remember what it was like before you knew Christ as Savior? Can you see the contrast between your life then and now? What could you possibly ask God for, which would require a greater miracle?

Paul describes the difference this miracle makes in us this way: "And you hath he quickened, who were dead in trespasses and sins; wherein in time past ye walked according to the course of this world, according to the prince of the power of the air, the spirit that now worketh in the children of disobedience: among whom also we all had our conversation in times past in the lusts of our flesh, fulfilling the desires of the flesh and of the mind; and were by nature the children of wrath, even as others. But God, who is rich in mercy, for his great love wherewith he loved us, even when we were dead in sins, hath quickened us together with Christ, (by grace ye are saved;) and hath raised us up together, and made us sit together in heavenly places in Christ Jesus: that in the ages to come he might show the exceeding riches of his grace in his kindness toward us through Christ Jesus. For by grace are ye saved through faith; and that not of yourselves: it is the gift of God: not of works, lest any man should boast" (Ephesians 2:1–9).

2. Creative prayer changes the way you view your past.

When you are born again the hurts of your past are not always automatically and instantly cured. Being born again is the initial treatment of an ailing life; it is not the total cure.

Many begin their Christian life with unpleasant memories from the past. Often these have left painful, deep marks on them. Such old hurts need to be healed so that we do not unconsciously—or perhaps, consciously—cling to them with all their pain. Unless we surrender old hurts, they get in the way of God's future for us in Christ.

While the facts of your personal history remain fixed, you can change the way you choose to feel and think about those facts. You can change the way you are affected by what has happened to you in the past. You don't have to be a prisoner of the facts of your past any longer.

Every year I talk to hundreds of believers who have brought with them into God's kingdom bitterness, disappointments, anger, fear, envy, jealousy, or other damaging feelings. Such pain may have its roots in things which have happened in their family, a former marriage, a job situation, or a church squabble. They may feel that their parents abused or mistreated them, their brothers and sisters were unfair to them, their former mate took advantage of them, a business partner cheated them, or people in the church gossiped about them. These are the kinds of things that fester in people's spirits.

What are the pains in your yesterdays which tend to spill over into your todays and threaten your tomorrows? How are you interpreting them? God can help you discover new and creative ways of viewing them through the options He stimulates in your mind by eternal life.

By choosing to see your old hurts in His way, you will become a better person rather than a bitter person. Notice, the difference between bitter and better is just one letter—"i." "I" make the difference between my becoming a bitter person or a better person by the way "I" choose to react to and think about the things which happen to me in life.

3. Creative prayer changes the way you view your external world.

It is amazing how different our external world looks once our internal world of remembrances and thoughts is comfortable. Many problems with others simply disappear. You see, problems between people usually have their roots in problems within people.

Back in the days when everybody hung their washing out on clotheslines, a dear lady used to complain about how dirty her neighbor's wash was—until the day she cleaned her own windows.

The internal perspective from which you view your world affects the way you see it. It also affects what you see. As in Israel's day (Numbers 13:33), when some people peer into the Promised Land of their tomorrows they see it full of giants so tall as to make them feel like grasshoppers. Others look at the same situation, discover a land that "flows with milk and honey," and are confident they can conquer it (Numbers 13:27,30).

When your thoughts about your present situation are stimulated by eternal life, you will know it. You will be thinking of your circumstances in the most positive way. A healthy person doesn't attempt to deal with the harsh realities of life by continually denying them. With God's help, he learns to view them as positively as possible. Often, these creative vantage points are revealed to the believer during times of prayer and meditation.

4. Creative prayer helps you change the external realities of your life.

God seldom performs miracles that affect men without involving men in the working of the miracles. I see many people who do not want to assume any responsibility for the circumstances in their lives. And, they feel so overwhelmed . . . they don't see how they can assume any responsibility for changing their circumstances.

They blame their unhappiness on others—their parents, their brothers and sisters, their friends, their mates, their former mates, their children, the devil. The list is endless. In their eyes, they are not responsible for what has happened to them and they are not able to do anything about it. Only God can deliver them!

This kind of passive-dependent person is a bystander in his own life! Someone has said there are basically three kinds of people in the world: people who make things happen, people who watch things happen, and people who never quite figure out what is happening.

Passive-dependent people never seem to get out of the grandstand in life. Usually they are fearful and angry— frightened of the responsibilities of life and angry at others for not doing more to help them.

Often, these people see their problems as the work of the devil. They insist that only the Lord can solve their problems. Satan causes them and Jesus takes them away while the person himself remains passive during the whole magical process. Unfortunately, the naive and indiscriminate believer frequently sees people who talk like this as being deeply spiritual. In most cases, nothing could be farther from the truth.

Eternal life is an invisible supernatural force, but it is not magic. In fact, the supernatural is neither magical nor superstitious. It is a dimension of reality in which God does His work in His world at levels of understanding beyond our comprehension. Isaiah expressed it this way, "For my thoughts are not your thoughts, neither are your ways my ways, saith the Lord. For as the heavens are higher than the earth, so are my ways higher than your ways, and my thoughts than your thoughts" (Isaiah 55:8,9).

Once we become aware of the impact of eternal life on our thought processes, God wants us to be involved with Him in the miracles that affect our lives.

Paul says it this way: ". . . work out your own salvation with fear and trembling: for it is God which worketh in you both to will and to do of his good pleasure" (Philippians 2:12,13). The fact that we are involved makes what happens no less supernatural. Paul assures us of this: "Now unto him that is able to do exceeding abundantly above all that we ask or think, according to the power that worketh in us" (Ephesians 3:20).

God never asks us to do what He knows we can't. As we

put the possible in His hand, He uses it to do the impossible. When Moses stretched out his rod toward the Red Sea, God parted the water. When Israel was willing to march around the walls of Jericho, God tore the walls down. When the servants at the marriage at Cana were willing to fill the waterpots with water, Jesus turned the water into wine. When one lad gave the Lord his five loaves and two fish, Jesus fed five thousand men plus the women and children.

People who just want to pray and let God do it all are exposing themselves to the risk of devastating disappointments.

Prayer alone seldom changes things

Prayer usually changes people—and people change things. Don't misunderstand. God can do all things. However, He has chosen us to become "workers together with him" (2 Corinthians 6:1). This is why God seldom performs a miracle which affects men without involving them.

By engaging in creative prayer, an ordinary person like you or I can learn how we can become involved with God in extraordinary manifestations of eternal life in our world.

How do you pray creatively?

First, commit God's Word to memory. How much Scripture do you know by memory? How long has it been since you have stored a new verse of God's Word in your mind? Remember, God's Word is creative. If you want your prayers to be creative you will want to involve both the living and written Word of God in them.

David found that hiding God's Word in his heart helped him build up an internal resistance to destructive attitudes and habits that sin would generate in his life. He wrote in Psalm 119:11, "Thy word have I hid in mine heart, that I might not sin against thee."

147

In addition to building up resistance to sin's destructive habits and attitudes, Scripture committed to memory becomes a creative resource which can surface at the proper moment to help you define options for living which otherwise would go undiscovered (John 14:26).

Second, spend time listening in prayer. For some people prayer is an exercise in one-way communication in which God does all the listening—and all the obeying. When they are finished talking to God, they are finished praying.

Yet, often in Scripture the believer is instructed to wait on God and to listen to God speak to him in return. In Revelation 2:7 Jesus admonishes, "He that hath an ear to hear, let him hear what the Spirit saith unto the churches. . . ." In Luke 8:18, He advises His disciples, "Take heed . . . how ye hear."

At first, when you start to listen in prayer, you may find it difficult to hear. So, let me suggest you begin by determining that you will spend half of your prayer time in listening. Just make that a standard practice of your prayer life. For example, if you are in the habit of spending ten minutes a day in prayer, then spend the first five minutes talking to God and the last five minutes letting Him talk to you.

When you begin to develop the art of listening in prayer, don't be surprised to discover a thousand voices filling the silence. The worries of yesterday, the cares of today, the fears of tomorrow all will try to come crashing in on you. Just as Paul explained, you will have to "study to be quiet" (1 Thessalonians 4:11).

Practice is essential if you are to develop this spiritual skill. However, in time the Lord will help you to become proficient in "casting down imaginations, and every high thing that exalteth itself against the knowledge of God, and bringing into captivity every thought to the obedience of Christ" (2 Corinthians 10:5).

Only as we learn to hear what God is saying to us in prayer do we begin to tap into the creative dimension of prayer. The psalmist learned this. He shares with us what the Lord taught him: "Be still, and know that I am God" (Psalm 46:10).

Americans are conditioned to a noisy life. When most of us wake up in the morning we turn on the radio or television to

148

provide our morning noise. In fact, some of us are wakened by the radio. Many of us cannot stand the stillness in our automobiles. No sooner do we get in the car and crank up the engine than we turn on the radio. The last thing turned off at night in many homes is the radio or television. So, from the time we get out of bed in the morning until we crawl back into bed at night, many of us demonstrate that we are more comfortable with noise than with silence.

Even in our churches there is very little silence. The organ is playing. Someone is singing. Someone is making announcements. The preacher is speaking. Many of us are so unaccustomed to silence in worship that we would find it extremely awkward. God wants us to seek out some quiet time. He urges us to develop the ability to listen to what the Spirit would say to us.

Mental fatigue is common among the people I see. They are bombarded with stimuli from waking to sleeping. Consequently, their ability to distinguish trivia from issues vital to their essential relationships is impaired. Millions of sights and sounds compete for their attention every day. People are mentally tired, even when their bodies are rested.

Few have learned how to rest their mind. One way of doing this is to develop the art of listening in prayer. Nothing is more restful and refreshing than quiet time before God. Isaiah discovered, "They that wait upon the Lord shall renew their strength; they shall mount up with wings as eagles; they shall run, and not be weary; and they shall walk and not faint" (Isaiah 40:31).

"Wait upon the Lord"

Meditation is one of the oldest forms of Christian worship and prayer. While Western Christianity has neglected this ancient tradition of the church, other religions are using it effectively as a means of attracting mentally tired Americans through the serenity which meditation offers. Today, meditation is so often associated with Eastern religions that some believers are reluctant to practice it. They fear that others might think they have abandoned their Christian faith.

However, Scripture makes it evident that God wants His people to enjoy the benefits of meditation. David describes the "blessed" or happy man as one whose "delight is in the law of the Lord; and in his law doth he meditate day and night" (Psalm 1:2).

Some of the most creative moments of my life have come after I have talked to God, praised Him, thanked Him, worshiped Him, and then sat quietly to listen to what He would say to me through His Spirit and from His Word. Once you have developed the ability to wait and listen, you won't want to pray without some time for meditation. For years, I have spent more time listening than talking in prayer.

If you are a beginner in learning to pray creatively, let me suggest that you take the first two or three minutes of your prayer time for quiet praise. Then, spend the next three or four minutes talking to God about your concerns. After that, rest your mind by committing all your cares to Jesus. Develop skill in following Peter's advice, "Casting all your care upon him; for he careth for you" (1 Peter 5:7). Focus your thoughts on a peaceful Bible scene or a restful verse of Scripture and wait quietly before the Lord.

Learn to take advantage of those unplanned moments that come to you by using them as opportunities for meditation. For example, most of us can get along very well with four and a half hours of deep sleep. Sometimes I wake up at 5:30 or 6 in the morning. I already have the hours of sleep I require. What am I going to do? I have several options. I can begin to wonder why it is I can't go back to sleep. I can become very upset and frustrated because someone or something has disturbed me early in the morning and robbed me of my sleep. Or, I can take advantage of this unexpected quiet time in the presence of the Lord and listen for what He may say to me.

Often in such moments the Lord will remind me of people to pray for. Or, He may bring to my attention certain situations that I need to take care of and help me to see them in ways I had not considered. Frequently, with such new perspectives the Lord also will suggest options for problem-solving that I had not thought of before. The wisdom He suggests to us in creative moments like these makes our smartest thoughts appear foolish.

It is at such times the Lord may show you new ways of feeling and thinking about some old hurts in your own life, and help you to change your views about people and events in your past which have caused you pain.

"It's all your fault!"

It was during such a sleepless night that God healed Jacob of the ill feelings he had had toward Esau (Genesis 32). Jacob was a great one for believing that his troubles were caused by others. So, as he was coming back home from his uncle Laban's, he remembered that he would soon have to meet his brother Esau. It had been years since the two had seen each other.

The last time Jacob was with his brother, Esau had threatened to kill him. If you remember how Jacob had collaborated with Rebekah to swindle Isaac's blessing from Esau, you can understand Esau's rage. Jacob believed Esau had kept that grudge alive for fourteen years.

So, Jacob concocted an elaborate scheme to make peace with his brother. He sent offerings of animals to Esau. Then he strategically arranged his servants, his wives, and even his children in a spectacular parade of appeasement. Each group had a carefully-prepared speech designed to convince Esau that Jacob considered himself to be Esau's servant.

Jacob was so afraid that after he had organized this gigantic parade, he sneaked off to spend the night on the other side of the brook. God sent an angel to confront him there and Jacob wrestled with him all night. As the dawn of Jacob's dreaded day began to break, the angel protested, "Let me go."

Jacob, afraid for his life, gripped the angel and cried, "I will not let thee go except thou bless me."

The angel responded by asking, "What is your name?" Jacob was being asked to honestly reflect on what characterized him, what defined his personality, and what behavior people who knew him had come to expect from him. This question forced Jacob to face the real source of his problems for the first time in his life. He could no longer blame them on his father, his mother, his brother, or his uncle. He had to confront the fact that he was

151

what his name implied—a deceiver and supplanter. After that night, Jacob would never be the same again. Finally, he faced the real source of his troubles—himself.

Notice what happened the morning after Jacob had that all-night wrestling match with the angel. When he faced Esau, who was it that made the first move toward whom? Who kissed whom first? It was Esau who threw his arms around Jacob. It was Esau who kissed Jacob.

Jacob discovered that Esau had forgiven him years before. Esau had put those painful differences that divided them behind him. It was Jacob who had harbored the grudge and kept it alive in his mind. Just think of the needless torture he had heaped upon himself through the years!

Ever since the fall of Adam we have tended to identify our own problems—but in other people. Children blame their problems on their parents. When divorce tears up a marriage, both partners tend to believe their divorce was mostly due to their mate's shortcomings or misbehavior. When people are fired, they explain it to themselves by accusing the supervisor of being unfair. Of course, there are rare instances in life where each of these explanations might be accurate. However, it is a creative miracle when God helps us to see that the problems we have with others are largely our own problems. And, the changes which need to take place are mostly ours to make.

If a person is ever to be happy (remember, that is what being "blessed" means), he must have the courage to face his problems as they really are. There comes a time for each of us when God confronts us with the same question the angel posed for Jacob: "What is your name?" In that moment, we need to face ourselves with the honesty portrayed in the old spiritual, "Not the preacher, nor the deacon, but it's me, O Lord, standin' in the need of prayer."

Creative prayer helps in problem solving

Creative prayer can help you discover new alternatives for solving the problems confronting you. It can also help you define new options for decisions you have to make.

In moments of meditation, learn to focus your thoughts on the matters demanding some judgment or decision from you. In each case, begin to define the options your own wisdom and experience suggest. In your imagination, project each of these options far enough into the future to anticipate its ultimate conclusion. If you are tuned in to your own thoughts during such a process you can hear yourself thinking, *If I were to do this, then that would happen. And then, that would follow. And then, that would take place.*

Pursue this same procedure with each option until as nearly as possible, you assess the consequences each of them would produce. Often, the Holy Spirit either will give you a fascination for an option you have defined through this process, or, through eternal life, He will stimulate one to your mind which had not previously occurred to you.

How will you know the difference between foolish thoughts which may surface in your mind during these moments of meditation and creative ways of viewing your situation which eternal life may stimulate? That distinction can be made more simply than you may imagine.

First of all, suggestions stimulated by eternal life are always consistent with Scripture.

Second, options stimulated by eternal life will improve your relations with the significant people in your life. God will never lead you to do anything that would destroy a Christian marriage or family. He will never lead you to do anything that would embarrass the body of Christ. He will never prompt you to be harmful to your neighbors or yourself. Any suggestions eternal life may introduce will be consistent with the most redemptive possible way of approaching the circumstances and relationships of your life.

Third, divine suggestions will lend themselves to making you more effective in doing what God has called you to do. God is glorified when you excel in the expression of the gifts and talents He has given you.

Fourth, whatever eternal life suggests is practical. It works! Often, when wisdom finally surfaces it is so obviously appropriate that we wonder why we didn't think of it sooner. However, never let the practicality of a creative suggestion diminish your appreciation of its supernatural origin. Some people can only see God in the spectacular. At times He does move in spectacular ways, but more often He moves through the regular channels of the routine matters of our lives.

As you develop an appreciation for God's guidance in the practical issues of your life you will be excited to discover how frequently you find Him there.

You can sort it all out!

It will take practice for you to develop skill in sorting out divine suggestions from the stream of your own thoughts. And, in the process you may do a foolish thing or two. Be patient with yourself. After all, that is a small price to pay for the thrill of experiencing divine guidance in your life.

The author of Hebrews reminds us that there are not many believers who are willing to take this risk; but, for those who will, there is the promise of improved skill in discernment with practice. "For when for the time ye ought to be teachers, ye have need that one teach you again which be the first principles of the oracles of God; and are become such as have need of milk, and not of strong meat. For every one that useth milk is unskilful in the word of righteousness: for he is a babe. But strong meat belongeth to them that are of full age, even those who by reason of use have their senses exercised to discern both good and evil" (Hebrews 5:12–14).

Here you are assured that as you practice the art of discerning good and evil in your thoughts, the Holy Spirit will help you become increasingly skilled in knowing which of your thoughts are the result of the confusion in and around you, which are the product of sin, which are the result of too much pizza before bedtime, and which are the creative voice of eternal life prompted by the Holy Spirit as He seeks to guide you in God's way.

Tomorrow's resources are unlimited!

The resources with which you face your tomorrows are not limited to the options of your own mind. Remember, you have

154

access to the mind of Christ that makes the wisdom of man look like foolishness (1 Corinthians 2:16); the unlimited power of eternal life that makes man's greatest strength look like weakness is at your disposal (1 Corinthians 1:25). Learning to draw from these resources in making major life decisions is a practical explanation of what walking in the Spirit is all about.

Remember when Peter was called of God to invite Gentiles into the kingdom? Peter felt he could never do that. He was a Jew, and naturally wanted the church to stay Jewish. If Peter had not been willing to put aside his personal bias, he would have missed that wonderful opportunity.

The biblical account is in the tenth chapter of Acts. There we are told that one day, while Peter was keeping his time of prayer, he drifted off to sleep. In that trance-like state between waking and sleeping, the Lord gave Peter one of the most creative moments of his life.

In a vision, Peter saw a large sheet let down from heaven. On it were all kinds of animals and birds. A voice said to Peter, "Kill and eat."

Peter responded with revulsion, "Lord, I am not about to touch anything on that sheet. There are all kinds of four-footed beasts and creeping things there. All my life no unclean thing has ever touched my lips."

Then, in that creative moment, the Lord said to Peter, "What I have cleansed is not for you to call common or unclean." A whole new dimension of ministry opened to Peter that day. He was wakened by a call from those who had come to take him to Cornelius's house so Gentiles could hear the gospel.

Down to the house of Cornelius Peter went. He couldn't even finish his gospel message to them before the Spirit of God fell on this group of Gentiles.

Back to the brethren at Jerusalem Peter came, saying, "What happened to us on the Day of Pentecost has happened to them!" It would have happened even if Peter hadn't gone, but Peter would have missed his chance to be a part of it. Because he was willing to involve himself in carrying out such a creative suggestion he had the thrill of seeing the gospel introduced to the Gentiles.

A new dimension of living for you!

I challenge you to become aware of the activity of eternal life in your thought processes. Look at prayer differently than you have before. Begin to spend at least as much time listening to God as you spend talking to Him.

If your todays are still suffering from yesterday's hurts, in prayer's quiet, creative moments let the Lord show you some healing ways to view your past. Nothing that has happened in your past needs to get in the way of God's best for your future.

Learn to identify the voice of the Lord in your thoughts. Involve His options in the problem-solving situations of your life. The decision-making opportunities of your tomorrows can be more exciting and challenging for you as you learn how to become involved with the Lord in the process of discovering His will. In those creative moments you have with Him, sharpen your skills in hearing what He is saying to you. And, "Whatsoever he saith unto you, do it" (John 2:5). As you do, you will discover yourself to be celebrating life in a new dimension.